Contents

Copyright
in school libraries

Fourth edition

Revised and updated by
Sandy Norman

Library Association Publishing
London

This fourth edition entirely supersedes the third edition published by Library Association Publishing in May 1996.

British Library Cataloguing in Publication Data
A catalogue record for this book is available from the British Library

ISBN 1-85604-326-6

Disclaimer

Typeset in 10/13pt Elegant Garamond and Humanist 521 by Library Association Publishing.
Printed and made in Great Britain by MPG Books, Bodmin, Cornwall.

Preface to the fourth edition

The main aims of this work, as with the other three editions, are to promote respect and understanding of copyright and to help library and information staff continue to provide a good service to their clientele whilst remaining on the right side of the law. Since the publication of the third edition of this guide, there have been major changes internationally and nationally, resulting from great pressure from rights holders for a tightening up of protection in the digital environment. This has led to the adoption of two new WIPO treaties and the publication of the draft EU directive dealing with copyright in the Information Society. Also, the UK Act has been changed as a result of the implementation of the EU Directive on Databases. All these changes will affect the library service and have to be assimilated by the library and information staff.

The format of this guide has not changed drastically from the previous edition but there are significant changes to the content. A new section giving an international background to intellectual property laws has been included, which will hopefully put copyright restrictions into perspective and give a greater awareness and understanding as to why the laws are drafted the way they are. A summary of the main provisions of the EU proposed Directive on Harmonization of Copyright and Related Rights in the Information Society has been included, as its importance to the future of the profession cannot be underestimated. Following the changes to the schools licences, this section has been expanded to cover the new conditions. There is a new section covering the database regulations, and the section covering electronic works has been expanded and updated in light of current thinking. New cases have been added to the case law section.

Acknowledgments

I would like to thank Ross Shimmon, Sue Brown, the ISD staff of the LA, and all the Members of the LA/JCC Working Party on Copyright, especially Frank Harris, Ray Wall and Graham Cornish, for all their help and support; and Barbara Schleihagen of EBLIDA and Emanuella Giavarra for their hard work on fighting the library cause in Europe. Above all I would like to thank the hundreds of librarians I have met or corresponded with over the past few years who have provided me with so many different copyright scenarios. The number of varied queries on copyright never ceases to amaze me.

Further advice

Library Association members who need further information on copyright matters are advised to contact Information Services at LAHQ in the first instance. If in-depth training is required, LA Continuing Professional Development (CPD) Department can arrange on-site training courses. Please contact Penny Simmonds. CPD also organizes regular training courses at LAHQ.

Introduction

These guidelines are intended mainly for library staff working in primary, secondary and special schools, and school library resource centres financed wholly or partially from public funds, and for librarians working in the independent sector. However, they will also be a useful source of information and guidance on copyright and licensing issues for teaching staff, ancillary staff, media resource technicians, reprographics staff and also volunteers working with information and media within the school environment.

There are separate guides available for libraries and information units in the FE and HE sector, public libraries, health libraries, libraries in the voluntary sector, and industrial and commercial libraries. These are also published by Library Association Publishing and details of how to obtain them are given on page 75.

This guide attempts to explain how the Copyright, Designs and Patents Act 1988, hereafter referred to as 'the Act', affects library and information staff and offers guidance on interpreting the main provisions of the law. Where appropriate, references are made to numbered sections of the Act, e.g. [S.29, S.41]. The contact details for organizations given in this guide will be found in Appendix C.

The Act took effect from August 1989 and applies throughout the UK. There have been several radical changes to the Act since then. Many of the definitions are scattered throughout the Act. Some of the terms are undefined, leaving them open to be dealt with by case law, agreement with copyright-owner representatives, or by common sense. The Act and relevant Statutory Instruments should be consulted for more detail when required. It should be borne in mind that the law, agreements with rights holders and licensing schemes are all subject to change. Any changes will be reported in the *Library Association record* and on the LA website (**http://www.la-hq.org.uk/lapublishing**).

The role of librarians and information professionals is to support the needs of their users to gain access to copyright works and the information and ideas contained within them. Although library staff cannot be expected to act as copyright police or as guardians of intellectual property, every effort should be made to protect and encourage respect for works under their control. Library and information staff could be seen to be encouraging copyright infringement if there appeared to be no barrier preventing infringing copies being made in the library resource centre or information unit. For instance, if there is a self-service photocopier in the library, it is extremely important that the advice given on page 62 – **Self-service copying machines and liability** – is heeded.

How to use this guide

The whole guide itself is intended to provide an easy-to-understand insight into copyright law from the point of view of the information intermediary and the users of information. It can be read by those who have limited or even no knowledge of copyright and wish to learn, and those who deal with copyright issues daily and wish to keep themselves up to date.

Care must be taken when copying and using copyright-protected material in schools. It is important that all staff working with books, journals, musical scores, audio and video material etc., are aware of the Act and the implications of infringement. It is essential, therefore, that all such staff should familiarize themselves with the following sections: **Guidance on the main provisions of the Act**, **Statutory changes since the 1988 Act**, **Exceptions to exclusive rights** (in particular fair dealing and the library regulations), **Guidance on copying limits** and **Guidance on digital copying**. Those involved in the management of licensing, especially the CLA scheme, will find this section useful. The rest of the guide can be dipped into when required.

New telephone codes

Telephone codes are changing during the lifetime of this Guide. The new codes have been given for all those numbers that are affected, as these will be operational from 1 June 1999. However, please note that before 22 April 2000, when dialling locally, you will need to use the existing local number. For example:

(0171) 636 7543 becomes (020) 7636 7543
From 1 June 1999, use (020) 7637 7543 when dialling from outside the old 0171 area but until 22 April 2000 use 636 7543 when dialling from inside the old 0171 area.

1 International basis of UK copyright laws

Berne Convention

Modern intellectual property laws are based on rights laid down by international conventions. The main copyright convention is the Berne Convention for the Protection of Literary and Artistic Works, to which most countries in the world are signatories. Under the terms of the Berne Convention, authors are entitled to some basic rights of protection for their intellectual output. National copyright laws are based on Berne. These basic rights laid down by Berne are translated into a set of restrictive acts which only the author, as creator, can authorize. The original agreement was drawn up in 1886 and since then there have been many revisions, each time increasing the scope of protection. However, not every original signatory signs up to a revision. Some are therefore signatories to one revision and others to another.

Berne recognizes society's need to access protected works and so allows exceptions and limitations to the exclusive rights. Under the terms of Article 9(2) of the Berne Convention, signatory nations are given the right to grant certain exceptions to the right of reproduction, within limitations:

> It shall be a matter for legislation in the countries of the (Berne) Union to permit the reproduction of such works in certain special cases, provided that such reproduction does not conflict with a normal exploitation of the work and does not unreasonably prejudice the legitimate interests of the author.

This is known familiarly as the Berne three-step test.

Universal Copyright Convention

Berne is complex, demanding a big commitment on the part of governments, and originally many countries in both developed and developing nations were unwilling or unable to sign up to all the conditions. In 1952 a compromise was reached with the Universal Copyright Convention, agreed at a UNESCO Conference in Geneva. The UCC established the use of the copyright symbol – ©. Most countries in the world are signatories to either the Berne Convention or the Universal Copyright Convention.

Conventions on neighbouring rights

There are two other important neighbouring rights conventions which give protection to performers and producers of a/v media. The International Convention for the Protection of Performing Artists, Producers of Phonograms and Broadcasting Organizations (Rome Convention) 1961 provides for the exclusive right of performers and broadcasters to authorize fixations of their performances and broadcasts respectively, as well as the exclusive right of reproduction for performers, phonogram producers and broadcasting organizations. This convention established the use of the familiar (P) symbol which accompanies the year or date of first publication. However, it has not had a successful history in attracting signatories. The Convention for the Protection of Producers of Phonograms against Unauthorized Duplication of their Phonograms (Geneva) 1971, familiarly called the Phonogram Convention, prevents unauthorized duplication of phonograms and was an attempt to strengthen the fight against piracy. The fear of piracy is behind many of the strict controls in countries where the phonographic industry is big business.

World Trade Organization and TRIPS

In 1994 the World Trade Organization Agreement was signed together with an annex to this agreement called TRIPS – the Trade Related aspects of Intellectual Property rights. The purpose of TRIPS was

> . . . to reduce distortions and impediments to international trade and . . . to ensure that measures and procedures to Intellectual Property rights do not themselves become barriers to legitimate trade.

The threat of trade sanctions meant that there was a greater incentive for countries to sign up to TRIPS, adopt stronger copyright laws and enforce protection. TRIPS signatories were obliged to comply with the main Articles of the Berne Convention.

WIPO

The United Nations organization responsible for managing the major international copyright conventions is the World Intellectual Property Organization (WIPO). Over several years a Committees of Experts debated a possible Protocol to the Berne Convention – in effect another revision; and a parallel committee discussed a proposal for a New Instrument (treaty) to give stronger protection to performers and producers of phonograms, thus updating the Rome and Phonogram Conventions and so hopefully making it more hospitable to more nations. There was growing pressure for WIPO to help resolve the problems caused by the impact of digital technology. In May 1996 , the WIPO discussions were concluded with the preparation of three treaties to be debated at a diplomatic conference in December 1996. Many of the new rights contained in TRIPS, such as protection for computer programs, compilations of data, and rental right, were incorporated into the WIPO proposals.

WIPO treaties

Two new copyright treaties were adopted: the WIPO Copyright Treaty and the WIPO Performers and Producers of Phonograms Treaty. The third proposal for a Database Treaty, which contained similar proposals to that already adopted by the EU, has not, at the time of writing (February 1999), been agreed.

As well as strengthening the rights of performers and record producers, the two new treaties added new rights. In the Copyright Treaty a new Right of Communication to the public was added which said that

> ... authors of literary and artistic works shall enjoy the exclusive right of authorizing any communication to the public of their works, including the making available by wireless or wireless means, in such a way that members of the public may access these works from a place and at a time individually chosen by them.

Library groups had no problem with this as long as exceptions could be allowed for legitimate practices. Because of the successful lobbying by such groups, provision was included in these treaties for signatory nations to allow new exceptions and limitations in their copyright laws which are appropriate to the digital environment, as well as affirming that existing exceptions applied to both the print and electronic environment.

Following the adoption of the two treaties, signatory nations are obliged to implement the new provisions into their own laws. In 1997, the EU put forward a proposal for a Copyright Directive: European Council Directive on the harmonization of certain aspects of Copyright and Related Rights in the Information Society. Included in the directive are proposals to 'harmonize' the exceptions to copyright. The Directive, which is very controversial, is causing concern amongst the library and information profession, and if the European Parliament cannot be persuaded to take a more balanced view, is likely to change the UK Act radically. At the time of writing, it has not yet been adopted by member states, so its effects are not likely to be seen until sometime after 2001. (See **Future changes** on page 29 for more information.)

2 Guidance on the main provisions of the Act

Materials subject to copyright

Copyright subsists in the following:

1 **Literary, dramatic, musical works**
   Literary works include tables or a compilations (other than a databases); computer programs; preparatory design material for computer programs; and databases. Dramatic works include works of dance or mime.
2 **Artistic works**
   Artistic works include photographs, maps, charts, plans, engravings, sculpture, and buildings or models of such.
3 **Sound recordings, films, broadcasts or cable programmes**
   Sound recordings include spoken word material. Films include any kind of video recording. Soundtracks are treated as part of a film.
4 **Typographical arrangements of published editions**
   This means the way the words are arranged on the pages of a literary, dramatic or musical work.

Criteria for protection

Copyright protection is automatic and there is no registration or other formality. For a literary, dramatic or musical work to qualify it must be original, i.e. not a facsimile copy of another work, and it has to be recorded, in writing or otherwise, regardless of whether the author has given permission for the recording or not. A sound recording or film only qualifies if it has not be taken from another sound recording or film.

The © symbol is not necessary for protection, although it is commonly used in published written works to draw the reader's attention to the holder of the rights in a work and the conditions of use. Any author concerned that their work may be misappropriated before publication may take precautions by depositing the work with their bank.

Length of the copyright period

From 1 January 1996, the duration of the copyright period was extended. One of the conditions of the extended term is that authors have to be European Economic Area (EEA) nationals. Please refer to SI 1995:3297 for exact conditions.

Literary, dramatic, musical or artistic works [S.12]

Copyright expires 70 years after the end of the year of a known author's death; *or* for works of unknown authorship, expiry is 70 years from the end of the calendar year in which the work was made, *or* 70 years from when the work was first made available to the public. 'Made available to the public' for a literary, dramatic or musical work includes publication, and the performance or inclusion of such works in a broadcast or cable programme service. For an artistic work, it includes being exhibited in public, being included in a film being shown to the public or being included in a broadcast or cable programme service. For works of joint authorship, the copyright expires 70 years following the last known person to die.

Photographs taken by whatever process on or after 1 August 1989 are protected for 70 years after the death of the photographer unless subject to Crown, Parliamentary or international organizations copyright (see below). If Crown copyright applies, protection is for a maximum of 125 calendar years unless they are published commercially, in which case they are protected for only 50 calendar years from the end of the year in which the photograph was created. Photographs subject to Parliamentary copyright are protected for 50 calendar years from taking. Photographs whose copyright belongs to any of the international organizations are protected for 50 calendar years from the end of the year in which the photograph was taken.

Crown, Parliamentary or international organizations [S.163–166, 168]

Protection for literary, dramatic, musical or artistic works protected by the Crown is for a maximum of 125 years. However, if during the first 75 years of that time such a work is published commercially, then protection by the Crown is for 50 years. For example, the copyright in Ordnance Survey maps exists for 50 years from the end of the year of publication. Works subject to Parliamentary and international organizations (e.g. UNESCO) copyright are protected for 50 calendar years.

Films [S.13B]

Copyright expires 70 years after the death of the last to die of the following: the principal director, the author of the screenplay, the author of the dialogue, or the composer of the music created for and used in the film.

Sound recordings [13A], broadcasts, cable programmes [S.14] and computer-generated works [S.12(7)]

Copyright expires 50 years after the end of the year in which they were made, released, or first broadcast or included in a cable programme service. A sound recording is *released* when it is first published, played in public, broadcast or included in a cable programme service. The latter term applies to services accessible via a public telecommunications system

Databases

For those databases which do not qualify for full copyright protection as compilations but do qualify for database right (see **Databases** on page 25), protection is given against unfair extraction and reutilization for 15 years.

Typographical arrangements of published works [S.15]

Copyright expires 25 years after the end of the year in which the edition was first published.

Who owns the copyright?

For literary, dramatic, musical or artistic works, the creator(s) of the work own(s) the copyright. This could be the author, artist, photographer, playwright, composer et al. In the case of computer-generated work, the author is the person who undertakes the arrangements necessary for the creation of the work.

Copyright is owned by the employer if the work is made in the course of employment, unless the contract specifies otherwise.

In the case of a sound recording or film, copyright is owned by the person who undertakes the arrangements necessary for the making of the recording (usually the producer) or film (usually the director, but see above for duration of copyright for **Films**); for broadcasts, it is the person who makes the broadcast; and in the case of a cable programme, the person who provides the service in which the programme is included. For databases it is the maker and for typographical arrangements of published works, it is the publisher.

It is important to note that those listed above are the initial owners of the copyright. These rights may be, and often are, assigned or sold to other persons or organizations. For example authors may assign all or some of their copyrights to a publisher.

What are rights and copyright infringement?

The owners of copyright have exclusive rights to their works. Anyone who does any of the activities below without permission or licence is infringing copyright apart from the specific exceptions allowed under the Act. Unless otherwise permitted or licensed, only rights holders are allowed the following:

1 **To copy the work [S.17]**

Copying means reproducing a work in any material form, and includes storing the work in any medium by electronic means. With regard to artistic works, it is also a restricted act to make a copy in three dimensions of a two-dimensional work, or make a copy in two dimensions of a three-dimensional work. It is also an infringement to make a copy which is transient or incidental to some other use of the work.

2 **To issue copies of the work to the public [S.18]**

This is the act of putting into circulation copies not previously put into circulation by or with the consent of the copyright owner and any subsequent distribution, sale, hiring or loan of copies, i.e. rental and lending.

3 **To perform, show or play the work in public [S.19]**

A performance includes delivery of a lecture, speech or sermon as well as a visual or acoustic presentation using a sound recording, film, broadcast or cable programme (this could be over an electronic network). Also, the playing or showing of the work in public is not allowed without permission.

4 **To broadcast the work or include it in a cable programme service [S.20].**

5 **To make an adaptation of the work or do any of the above in relation** to the adaptation **[SS.16–21]**

This means adapting a literary, dramatic or musical work into a different format, e.g. from a novel into a play, or making a translation from one language to another. It also applies to altering or changing the arrangement of computer program or databases.

Doing any of the above, innocently or otherwise, without the licence of the copyright owner, constitutes a breach of copyright, which is usually referred to as *primary infringement*. Anyone who authorizes another to commit primary infringement is also liable. Infringement can occur only if the whole or a 'substantial part' is involved. However, although undefined in the Act, this has been established by case law as turning upon significance of content as well as extent. Therefore almost anything could be judged 'substantial' in particular circumstances. For example, copying a two-page summary and recommendations of a 100-page report may be judged substantial in certain cases. Similarly, copying a segment of a photograph or a detail from some other form of artistic work may also be regarded as a 'substantial part'. A substantial part may also depend on skill and originality. Although there is no copyright in an idea, if in producing a new work for commercial publication, an author makes (unacknowledged) excessive use of someone else's written ideas, he/she may be accused of infringement even though none of it was actually reproduced. In a dispute, it would be up to the court of law to decide how much skill and originality was used by the author. In addition to primary infringement, certain other acts performed without the consent of the rights holder, by people knowing or having reason to believe that they may be infringing acts, may be classed as *secondary infringements*.

Secondary infringement [SS.22–26]

Unless specific permission is granted, it is not permitted to import infringing copies into the UK (other than for private or domestic use). The Act also forbids possession in the course of business, selling, hiring (or offering to do so), or otherwise distributing infringing copies to such an extent that it damages the copyright owners' entitlement.

An important point to note is that a copy made for a purpose allowed under the Act can automatically become an infringing copy if used in other circumstances. For example, a copy quite legitimately made for an examination question could become an infringing copy if used for another purpose [S.27] or a photocopy made by a librarian where the librarian knew, or had reason to believe, that the declaration was false could be an infringing copy.

It is an infringement to provide the means specifically designed for making infringing copies, if it is known (or there is a reason to believe) that it will be used to make infringing copies. An obvious example would be a set of printing plates to print banknotes.

Without the licence of the copyright owner, it is an infringement to transmit a work by means of a telecommunications system (otherwise than by broadcasting or inclusion in a cable programme service) while knowing or having reason to believe that infringing copies of the work will be made by the recipients of the transmission.

Persons may be liable for infringement if they permit premises to be used, or provide equipment, for an infringing performance of a copyright literary, dramatic or musical work, unless there are grounds for believing that the performance will not infringe. This refers to the playing of sound recordings, the showing of films (videos) or the receiving visual images or sounds conveyed by electronic means.

Moral rights

Moral rights belong to authors and are independent of the economic rights of copyright. It is important to be aware of them as they become increasingly relevant in the digital environment. The four moral rights are:

1 **The right of paternity** is the right of the author to be identified as such. This right has to be asserted and a statement to this effect is to be found on the title page verso of many publications and on the backs of photographs or the mounts of transparencies or slides. There are exceptions to this right, e.g. the right does not apply to computer programs, design of typefaces and computer-generated works. Nor does it apply to works generated in the course of employment [S.77–79].

2 **The right of integrity** is the right of the author to prevent or object to derogatory treatment of his/her work [S.80]. *Treatment* is defined to mean an addition, deletion from, alteration to or adaptation of the work. (Adaptation in this sense does not apply to a translation of a literary, dramatic or musical work.) The treatment of a work

would be seen as *derogatory* if it is distorted or mutilated, or is otherwise seen as being prejudicial to the honour or reputation of the author. This is extremely relevant for works in digital format, especially artistic works, which can be easily manipulated. However, this moral right was first introduced in the 1988 Act, so does not strictly apply to works created before then.

3 **The right of false attribution** is the right of persons not to have a literary, dramatic, musical or artistic work falsely attributed to them [**S.84**].

4 **The right of disclosure** is the right of the author to withhold certain photographs or films from publication. Under the UK Act this would apply to a person who commissions the work but decides not to have it issued to the public, exhibited or shown in public, or included in a broadcast or cable programme [**S.85**].

Remedies for infringement [SS.107–115]

Rights holders are able to protect their rights through civil as well as criminal courts. Rights holders are thus able to institute proceedings against alleged infringement in the Magistrates' Courts rather than the High Court. The choice will depend on the seriousness of the infringement and how quickly an infringer must be dealt with. If civil proceedings are issued, a rights holder has more control and may act quickly. The drawback from their point of view is that they have to fund the proceedings. Criminal liability applies mainly to deliberate infringement for commercial gain, i.e. piracy. It is the police or local trading standards officers who initiate these proceedings. The most likely penalties for infringing copyright are: (a) an injunction to prevent further infringement; (b) an instruction to 'deliver up' infringing copies to the rights holders; and (c) the award of damages. This could be an amount equivalent to the profits the rights holder would otherwise have made on any of the infringer's sales. Similar penalties and procedures apply under Scottish law.

NB Where an offence is committed by a body corporate is proved to have been committed with the consent or connivance of a director, manager, secretary or other similar officer of the body, or a person purporting to act that capacity, he/she is guilty of the offence and liable to be proceeded against and punished. [**S.110**]

3 Exceptions to exclusive rights

There are 47 specific exceptions in the UK Act, only some of which are covered in this and the following chapters. The main exceptions (also called *permitted acts* or *statutory provisions*) relevant to the library and information profession are: a general right to copy called fair dealing; copying for educational purposes; and copying by librarians and archivists. These are outlined in detail in this chapter.

Fair dealing

Fair dealing is an undefined term which does not in itself give specific permission to copy. It is really a defence that could be used by a person accused of infringement if the case were taken to court. Fair dealing only applies to specific purposes: research or private study; criticism or review; or news reporting. *Dealing*, in this sense, is a form of general behaviour. What is *fair* could only be decided in court in respect of specific circumstances and works. It is taken to mean, however, that *fair* dealing would not unfairly deprive rights holders of a reasonable financial return on their intellectual property.

Most copying in schools will be covered by a licence from the Copyright Licensing Agency, although the following may apply to copying works which are excluded from the licence, or to copying outside the school premises e.g. in a public library.

Fair dealing: research or private study [S.29]

The Act says that 'fair dealing with a literary work other than a database, or a dramatic, musical or artistic, for the purposes of research or private study does not infringe any copyright in the work.' Nor does it infringe copyright in the typographical arrangements of a published edition.

Private study is undefined, but it is obviously intended to exclude group or class study; and *research* (apart from databases) covers any kind, including that undertaken for commercial or industrial purposes. With regard to (copyright-protected) databases, fair dealing applies as long as the source is indicated and the research is not for a commercial purpose: 'the doing of anything in relation to a database for the purposes of research for a commercial purpose is not fair dealing with the database.' [S.29(5)]

The amount that may be copied is not specified, nor is the number of copies. However, if a person copies on another's behalf, only one copy may be made. Any library may also copy on behalf of an individual under this provision (as well as under the library regulations) but a librarian must not use fair dealing in order to copy more. [S.29(3)] Librarians are not allowed to make multiple copies under the provisions of the library regulations, so it follows that the same applies to fair dealing for research or private study. Fair dealing includes artistic works, whereas the library regulations do not. The Library Association recommends that copying under fair dealing for research or private study should observe the same limits set down by the library regulations. Anyone copying on behalf of someone else for research or private study is restricted to making one copy. Persons copying for themselves do not appear to be so restricted, but may have to defend 'fairness' to the copyright owner. It is advised, therefore, that unless there is good reason, only single copies should be made.

Fair dealing: criticism or review [S.30(1)]

Anyone may copy from any type of work for the purposes of criticism or review provided sufficient acknowledgement is given. It is implied that making multiple copies for publication (e.g. a quotation) for this purpose is permitted. Although no amounts are given in the Act, the generally accepted limits for quotations are: one extract of no more than 400 words; several extracts none more than 300 words and totalling no more than 800 words; or up to 40 lines from a poem (this should not exceed more than one-quarter of the whole poem). Permission is not given explicitly to copy the typographical layout under this provision. It cannot be assumed that copying an artistic work by one author whilst criticizing or reviewing the work of another is acceptable either, unless there is an obvious, necessary and direct link between them. In other words, genuine comparison of artistic works is acceptable, while merely generically illustrative or visually exciting use of photography or film, depicting, say, one version of a play or operatic production whilst commenting on a new presentation of the same, is not.

Fair dealing: current events [S.30(2)]

Anyone may copy from a work (but not photographs) for the purposes of reporting current events, provided sufficient acknowledgement of the source is given. No acknowledgement is required for reporting done by means of a sound recording, film, broadcast or cable programme. It is implied that making multiple copies for publication (e.g. a quotation) for this purpose is permitted. It cannot be assumed, however, that it is acceptable to copy the typographical layout under this provision as no explicit permission is given.

Incidental inclusion [S.31]

If a copyright work is included incidentally in an artistic work, sound recording, film, broadcast or cable programme, copyright is not infringed. An example of this might be the making of a video in which a work of art was on display.

Copying by librarians and archivists [SS.37–43]

On 1 August 1989, regulations came into force for librarians and archivists (and those acting on their behalf). These regulations (SI 1989:1212), known as the 'library regulations' or 'library privileges', apply to library staff who carry out photocopying on behalf of their users and for other libraries. **For users copying on self-service photocopiers, the fair dealing notes apply** (see above).

It is important to note that the regulations apply to the copying of literary, dramatic or musical works but not artistic, although an illustration may be copied if it accompanies a work. Permission to copy under these provisions also includes copying the typographical arrangement. Librarians who provide a staffed photocopying service are obliged under the Act to provide photocopy declaration forms for users to sign. A copy of the prescribed declaration form is given in Appendix B (this form may be copied freely). Librarians must be satisfied that these declaration forms are valid, insofar as this is possible, which throws responsibility on library staff. However, staff cannot be expected to check records retrospectively. The LA therefore considers that recognition of duplicate requests must be left to the memory of the staff concerned. However, the Act implies that librarians will act responsibly and it is important to make a positive effort to reflect this trust. Note the following:

1 Any UK library can act as an intermediary, and make and supply copies in response to research or private study requests from individuals via other libraries.
2 Profit-based libraries or archives are prescribed to copy for other libraries under **SS.41, 42** and **43**, but may not receive copies for their own stock.
3 Non-profit-based libraries outside the UK are prescribed for receiving copies made for them by a UK library under **SS.41** and **42**.
4 Any UK library, including a profit-based service, can copy on behalf of individuals under fair dealing [**S.29**].

Copying service (local or interlibrary document supply) [SS.38–40]

Librarians and archivists may provide a copying service, in response to local or interlibrary requests from individuals, subject to the conditions below. **NB** Copying must be for the purposes of research or private study only, and *research* embraces all kinds of research, including commercial research, while *private study* excludes class or group study.

The requirements are as follows:

1 The requester must sign a form declaring that

- a copy of the same material has not previously been supplied by any librarian
- the material is for the purposes of research or private study only
- the requester is not aware that any other person has requested, or is about to request, a copy of substantially the same material for substantially the same purpose.

2   The librarian must not accept requests for substantially the same material at substantially the same time (these terms are not defined).

3   No more than one copy of an article per periodical issue, or no more than a reasonable proportion from a published work, may be requested.

4   The librarian must make a charge for the copy to recover the costs of production, together with a contribution towards the general expenses of the library (see **Charging for copying** on page 54).

The librarian must be satisfied that the information on declaration forms is not false and that the request is valid. The reason behind all the bureaucracy is to prevent systematic single copying whereby several people make requests for the same items at about the same time. For example, if several pupils asked for the same item for the same project, it should not be supplied under the library regulations. This is why schools have to have a CLA licence.

Interlibrary copying for stock [S.41]

Librarians are allowed to request items from another library to add to their collection provided that the conditions are met. Copies may not be made from the library's own collection under this exception. The regulations state that librarians are permitted to make and supply to a non-profit-based library 'a copy of any article in a periodical' or, as the case may be, 'of the whole or part of a published edition' of a literary, dramatic or musical work for stock required by that other library, subject to the following conditions:

1   The requesting library must not be furnished with more than one copy of the same article or of the whole or part of the published edition.

2   Where the request is for more than one article from a periodical, or the whole or part of a published edition, the requesting library must satisfy the librarian (in a *written* statement) that that they do not know, and are unable to find out, the name and address of the person or persons who could authorize the copying (e.g. for an out-of-print item whose publisher is no longer in business).

3   The librarian must make a charge for the copy to recover the costs of production, together with a contribution towards the general expenses of the library.

It follows that where the request is for only one copy of an article, and for less than the whole or (a substantial) part of a published work, there is no requirement to obtain written permission. Copies required for library stock may be obtained from the BLDSC or from any other library. Copies obtained for stock, **even though they are photocopies**, are legitimate copies and may be placed in the library collection, lent out, or copied under fair dealing.

Copying for replacement [S.42]

School librarians may also make copies of items in their permanent collections in order to preserve or replace them by replacing the copy in the permanent collection in addition to or in place of it. This means that if the library wishes to withdraw an item because of actual or potential damage, provided the conditions are met, it may substitute that item with a copy. Copies may also be made for other prescribed libraries or archives which have suffered a loss or damage. The conditions are as follows :

1   The item must be held in the permanent collection for reference only, or must be held in the permanent collection and made available for loan only to other libraries for reference purposes.
2   It must not be reasonably practical for the item to be purchased.
3   If the copy is for another library, then the other library must declare in a *written* statement
    • that the copy has been lost, destroyed or damaged
    • that it is not reasonably practical to purchase a replacement
    • that the copy will be for reference purposes only.
4   The librarian must make a charge for the copy to recover the costs of production, together with a contribution towards the general expenses of the library.

Example 1: A book has been severely defaced. The library wishes to replace it and writes to another library for a copy, declaring that it has been lost and that the book is no longer available for purchase. The copy is supplied and put in the reference collection.
Example 2: Several newspaper issues are falling to bits. They are no longer available for purchase, so the librarian may copy all of them (maybe on microfiche) to keep them in the permanent collection.

Copying unpublished works [S.43]

Librarians of non-profit-based libraries are also allowed to copy the whole or part of certain unpublished literary, dramatic or musical works from documents held in the library or archive, subject to the following conditions:

1 The requester must sign a form declaring that
  - a copy of the same material has not previously been supplied by any librarian
  - the material is for the purposes of research or private study only
  - the requester is reasonably sure that the document has not been published prior to being deposited in the library or archive, and that the copyright owner has not prohibited the copying of the work.
2 Only one copy may be supplied to the requester.
3 The librarian must make a charge for the copy to recover the costs of production, together with a contribution towards the general expenses of the library.

The most important thing to remember about copying unpublished works is that permission must be obtained from the author before copying. A special declaration form is necessary for copying unpublished works (not the one given in Appendix B), a copy of which may be found in the library regulations (SI 1989:1212).

Special rules for education [S.32–35]

Copying for instruction [S.32]

The Act says that it is permitted to copy from a literary, dramatic, musical or artistic work in the course of instruction or preparation for instruction, provided it is done by the person giving or receiving instruction, and not copied by means of a reprographic process. A *reprographic process* is defined as a process for making facsimile copies, or which involves the use of an appliance for making multiple copies. This indicates that copying from copyright material for class purposes is only allowed if it is done in long-hand and not on a photocopier.

   If an educational establishment is licensed, then multiple photocopying for class use is allowed, subject to the restrictions of the licence. If no licence is available, teachers may copy 1% of any work in any quarterly period, i.e. 1 January–31 March, 1 April–30 June etc. [S.36]. This exception could apply to those works excluded from the CLA licence, for example.

Copying for examinations [S.32(3)]

The Act says that it is not an infringement to copy for the purposes of examination by way of setting the questions, communicating the questions to the candidates, or answering the questions apart from the reprographic copying of a musical work for use by an examination candidate in performing the work. 'Purposes of examination' is not defined but it is unlikely that this exemption applies to work continuously assessed as part of the examination process. Copies made for this purpose must not be subsequently 'dealt with', otherwise they become infringing copies. This means that subsequent commercial publication or distribution of collections of past examination papers, or extracts from them containing parts of copyright material, would be illegal unless permission were obtained.

Performing a literary, dramatic or musical work [S.34]

Permission is also given to educational establishments to perform a literary, dramatic or musical work and to play or show a sound recording, film or video, broadcast or cable programme to audiences of lecturers and students 'in the activities of the establishment or for the purposes of instruction' (see **Videos** on page 64). Permission must be sought from rights holders if a performance is to be public (see also **Playing music in educational establishments** on page 60). **NB** Artistic works do not need permission because their display or exhibition does not infringe copyright.

Off-air recording [S.35]

Off-air recording from broadcasts or cable programmes (radio and television) may be made by or on behalf of an educational establishment without infringing copyright unless there is a licensing scheme available. At present there are two licensing schemes (please see page 40 for details). Satellite and cable channels, provided they are legitimately received, may be recorded for educational purposes as there is no licensing scheme available.

4 Other exceptions and permissions

The most important exceptions which apply to the library and information profession are covered in detail in the previous chapter, but there are others which the profession needs to be aware of. Here is a selection of the most relevant.

Parliamentary and judicial proceedings [S.45]

Copyright is not infringed by copying for the purposes of Parliamentary or judicial proceedings. In the case of judicial proceedings this is generally accepted to refer to copying only after the issuing of a writ.

Royal Commission or statutory enquiry [S.46]

Copyright is not infringed by anything done for the purposes of the proceedings of a Royal Commission or statutory enquiry.

Public inspection [S.47]

Material open to public inspection for statutory purposes (e.g. planning documents lodged with a local authority, or electoral registers) may be copied, subject to certain conditions.

Anonymous or pseudonymous works [S.57]

Copying is allowed from a literary, dramatic, musical or artistic work if, after reasonable enquiry, it proves impossible to ascertain the identity of the author (or authors if there is joint authorship), and where it is reasonable to assume the copyright has expired or that the author, or authors died over 70 years ago. This does not apply to works protected by the Crown or international organizations (see **Seeking copyright permission** on page 00).

Reading in public [S.59]

The reading or recitation in public by one person of a reasonable extract from a published literary or dramatic work does not infringe copyright if it is acknowledged. It would be wise to obtain permission from the publishers in the case of formally organized events as opposed to informal readings.

Abstracts [S.60]

Abstracts which accompany scientific or technical articles in periodicals may be copied and issued to the public, unless there is a licensing scheme available. No licensing scheme exists at present. Abstracts contained in abstracting bulletins are not covered by this exception.

Advertising art works for sale [S.63]

Copies may be made and issued to the public of artistic works in order to advertise them for sale. This would include the compilation of such works in a catalogue.

Playing of sound recordings in clubs [S.67]

Clubs or societies which are not conducted for profit, and whose main objects are charitable or otherwise concerned with the advancement of religion, education or social welfare, are allowed to play sound recordings, provided any charge for admission is applied solely for the purposes of the organization.

Off-air recording for time-shifting purposes [S.70]

The private and domestic copying of a broadcast or cable programme (i.e. making a video of a TV programme, or a tape of a radio programme, for use at a more convenient time) is allowed. This is familiarly called time-shifting. This provision does not apply to schools (see **Off-air recording licensing schemes** on page 40).

Photograph of a television broadcast or cable programme [S.71]

A photograph or slide may be made of the whole or part of an image forming part of a television broadcast or cable programme for private and domestic use.

Free public showing or playing of a broadcast or cable programme [S.72]

As long as the public is not charged for admission to wherever the showing is to take place, this is allowed. This mainly applies to clubs or societies which are not run for profit or residents and inmates of a building.

5 Statutory changes since the 1988 Act

Following the publication of a Green Paper in 1988, the Commission of the European Communities embarked on a programme to harmonize the various copyright laws of member states. The areas where harmonization was seen to be necessary were: computer programs, the term of protection, rental and lending and certain neighbouring rights, databases, private copying, satellite and cable broadcasting, and moral rights. The following is a selection of those amendments relevant to the library and information profession which have been implemented within the UK Act.

Computer programs

The law relating to computer programs was the subject of the first amendment to the 1988 Copyright Act. It was amended by SI 1992:3233 The Copyright (Computer Programs) Regulations 1992 to comply with EU Directive No. 91/250/EEC on Computer Software. Computer programs are protected as literary works, which gives them the full protection of the Berne Convention. The UK already protected computer programs, but the Directive allowed certain exceptions which were absent from the 1988 Act. The changes mean that a lawful user of a copy of a computer program is allowed

- to make a back-up copy even if terms or conditions state otherwise
- to copy or adapt it, provided that the copying or adapting is necessary for lawful use and is not prohibited under contract
- to observe, study or test a program by any device or means
- to decompile the program to the extent necessary to achieve the interoperability of an independently created program with other programs.

The definition of a lawful user of a computer program is a person who has a right to use the program, whether by licence or otherwise. The back-up copy made may be used to replace the original if it is corrupted and the program needs to be restored, or if the software goes missing. In the case of books with accompanying software, if the software is stolen or goes missing, a lawful user may make a further copy to replace the missing disk.

When purchasing computer software packages, schools should consider the appropriate multi-user licence needed. Without such a licence, the software may be loaded onto one machine only. The use of unlicensed software can be a civil or criminal offence. Every time unlicensed software is run, an infringement takes place. Major software development companies are increasingly concerned about illegal copies of their software which are being made and distributed to large companies and so defrauding them of large sums of revenue. They estimate that 'piracy' is costing their industry millions of pounds per annum. FAST – Federation Against Software Theft – was formed to combat this piracy. The Business Software Alliance is also extremely active in this area. Without prior warning, premises which are suspected of holding or using illegal software can be raided. Criminal proceedings can be started leading to hefty damages. Several companies have been prosecuted successfully.

Extension of the term of protection

EC Directive 93/98/EEC on the Duration of Copyright directed member states to extend the term of protection for copyright literary, dramatic, musical and artistic works and films from 50 to 70 years after the year of the death of the author. This became law in the UK on 1 January 1996 with the Duration of Copyright and Rights in Performances Regulations SI1995:3297.

For existing works still in copyright on 31 December 1995, copyright protection was extended for a further 20 years. Works for which copyright expired before 31 December 1995 in the UK, but which were still protected in another EU member state on 1 July 1995, had their copyright revived. Depending on the year of the author's death, this meant protection was extended for up to another 20 years. The owner of the extended copyright is the person who owned the copyright before 1 January 1996. The owner of the revived copyright is the person who owned the copyright immediately before it expired. The last owner of the rights could belong the author's estate, a literary estate or assigned to a publisher.

Anyone who copied or published works which were once in the public domain and which had their copyright revived were treated as having been licensed by the copyright owner subject to agreed payments of a reasonable royalty or remuneration. There was no requirement to pay remuneration or royalty where innocent copying which did not involve publication was undertaken by a user.

Rental and lending right

The Act of 1988 established a new and separate right for rental services [S.18], and rental included public lending. Public lending right is now separated from rental right with the Copyright and Related Rights Regulations 1996 (SI 1996:2967), which implemented the European Council Directive on Rental and Lending No 92/100/EEC. Lending is defined as making a copy of a work available for use on terms that it will or may be returned, otherwise than for a direct or indirect or commercial advantage through an establishment which is accessible to the public. Whereas public libraries are obviously subject to the new rules, schools, along with other educational establishments, are exempt from any lending restriction. [**S.36A**]

Publication right

In Council Directive No. 93/98/EEC (the Duration Directive) a new right was given to works, i.e. literary, dramatic, musical, artistic work or a film, in which copyright has expired and which have not previously been published. Called publication right, it was implemented into the UK Act as part of SI 1996:2967 The Copyright and Related Rights Regulations 1996. Publication right lasts for 25 years, has the protection in the same way as other newly created works and is subject to the same provisions. Sound recordings will not attract publication right and the right does not apply to expired Crown or Parliamentary copyright material.

The definition of *publication* is very broad and includes any communication to the public, in particular: issuing copies to the public, making the work available by an electronic retrieval system; rental and lending to the public; performing, exhibiting or showing the work in public; or broadcasting the work or including it in a cable programme service. In order to publish a work, a publisher must be authorized to do so. Permission must be obtained from the owner of the 'physical medium on which the work is embodied.' Works which are published without authorization would not qualify for this right. In order for a publisher to qualify for this right, he/she must be an EEA national at the time of publication and the work must be first published in an EEA state.

It is likely that this right will have little effect on libraries and archives, as most copyright-expired material in libraries would already have been made available to the public and therefore technically published. Also, most unpublished material will still be in copyright until 2039 at least. Therefore, the only materials which are likely to be affected are very old works. Some very old photographs and other documents in local studies collections which are not on open inspection (over 150 years old at least) may fall into these categories. However, the third hurdle is that potential publishers are obliged to ask the owner (or keeper) for permission to use their material. This could be refused if felt necessary. Also, there could be a problem if publication right was asserted erroneously, as there does not appear to be any sanction for false assertion. There may be many naïve owners who may be misled by unscrupulous predatory publishers. Librarians and archivists should be aware of these implications, as there are no misrepresentation remedies or get-out clauses in the regulations.

Databases

After discussions spanning four years, the controversial European Council Directive No. 96/9/EC on the legal protection of databases was adopted and has now been implemented by SI 1997:3032 The Copyrights and Rights in Database Regulations 1997. The

Directive introduced a new form of property protection for databases to prevent unfair extraction and reutilization of their contents. The Government is aware of potential problems and has set up a Database Marketing Strategy Group to monitor the impact of the changes on the education, library and publishing sectors. Reports on the progress of this group will be announced by the Patent Office and will be reported in the *LA record* and on the LA website.

Although the original 1988 Act included protection for databases, the word *database* was never mentioned or defined. It was covered by the term *compilation*. The definition given of a database is broad and includes any structured collection, whether in print or electronic format, of works, data or other material arranged in a systematic or methodical way and which are individually accessible by electronic or other means. Collections of data include directories, encyclopaedias, statistical databases, online collections of journals and multimedia collections. Webpages and other collections of data on the Internet are also covered.

Full copyright protection will now only be given to those databases (compilations) which by virtue of their selection and arrangement of the contents constitute the author's own 'intellectual creation'. A compilation which does not meet the originality criteria for copyright protection can now only be protected by a new right called database right. However, *any* database may qualify for database right as long as a substantial investment has been made in the obtaining, verification and presentation of their contents by the database maker. So, although a database must be original to qualify for copyright, it need not be original to qualify for database right. All this is regardless of the actual *contents*, which may or may not have copyright protection in their own right.

Database right has a basic term of protection against unfair extraction and reutilization of the contents, and expires 15 years after the end of the calendar year in which the database was made. However, any substantial change to the database during this time (additions, deletions or alterations) which results in substantial additional investment will give rise to a further 15-year extension. Just how extensive these changes have to be before the database deserves a further term is not known. It is likely that many dynamic databases will be protected indefinitely.

Protection is only given to EEA nationals or those whose residence, central administration or principal place of business is in the EEA. The legislation came into force on 1 January 1998 and affects those databases created on or after that date, except that for those databases which because of the new regulations will now only have database right protection, and which were completed on or after 1 January 1983, receive the 15-year protection commencing 1 January 1998.

The Government made it clear, during the consultation process, that it had no wish to change the present exceptions other than required by the precise wording of the EC Directive. Consequently there are few changes to the copying allowances for databases with the full copyright protection, but any changes are major ones and will have important repercussions, especially for the commercial and industrial sectors.

Exceptions allowed for copyright databases

The EU laid down in the directive that an exception for copying for a commercial purpose should not be allowed. Therefore, exceptions which allow general fair dealing
copying have to be amended to comply with this. The UK law has not, until now, dis-
tinguished between academic, scientific and commercial research. Any research which
is for a commercial purpose will not now be considered to be fair dealing. S.29(1) of the
CPDA 1988, copying under fair dealing for research or private study, is therefore
amended. This section now reads:

> Fair dealing with a database for the purposes of research or private study does not infringe any
> copyright in the database provided that the source is indicated . . . the doing of anything in
> relation to a database for the purpose of research for a commercial purpose is not fair dealing
> with the database.

There are no other amendments to the exceptions which allow copying in libraries, education and other miscellaneous provisions so it is assumed these will still apply. It follows that copying for a user under the library regulations will not be subject to the non-
commercial research qualification. Whether this was deliberate or an oversight is not
known.

Exceptions under database right

Exceptions are given for lawful users. A lawful user is described as any person who
(whether under a licence to do any of the acts restricted by any database right or otherwise) has a right to use the database. The LA believes that a lawful user could be: any
purchaser of a printed database; any purchaser of a 'portable database' (e.g. CD-ROM);
any licensed user of an electronic database; and any client of an information service or
library which is a lawful user.

Lawful users of a database are authorized to do anything necessary to enable them
to access and use the contents. The regulations state that

> it is not an infringement of copyright in a database for a person who has a right to use the data-
> base or any part of the database (whether under licence to do any of the acts restricted by the
> copyright in the database or otherwise)i.e. a lawful user to do, in the exercise of that right, any-
> thing which is necessary for the purposes of access to and use of the contents of the database
> or of that part of the database.

It is also stated that, even if there is a term or condition in any contract which accompanies the database which purports to prohibit or restrict this lawful use, this can be
ignored.

It is an infringement of database right if someone extracts and reutilizes a *substantial* part of the contents without authorization. However, lawful users are allowed to extract or reutilize *insubstantial* parts of a database which has been made available to the public in any manner. **NB** Repeated or systematic extraction or reutilization of insubstantial parts could amount to a substantial part and thus be an infringement. Also, the regulations state that for avoidance of doubt, any term or condition in any agreement (licence) to use such a database which prevents such extraction or reutilization shall be void.

An exception is given for extracting a *substantial part* of the contents for fair dealing if the extraction is undertaken by a lawful user and 'it is extracted for the purpose of illustration for teaching or research and not for any commercial purpose'. The source must also be indicated. **NB** This exception only covers extraction not reutilization. The term 'illustration for teaching or research' is new to the UK and has been extracted straight from the Directive, possibly because the Government was reluctant to define what it actually means in practice. *Reutilization* covers all forms of making contents available, whether in print or electronic fixed media, online transmission, or broadcasting etc., so extracting is likely to mean merely displaying on screen Therefore, it could mean that a substantial part may be copied or displayed on a screen for teaching or non-commercial research purposes, but must not be reused (presumably to prevent the unauthorized creation of a new database). How this would apply to a printed database is not known. How one is able to distinguish between commercial and non-commercial is also unclear.

Exceptions are included to cover copying for Parliamentary and judicial proceedings; Royal Commission and statutory enquiries; material open to public inspection or on an official register; material communicated to the Crown in the course of public business; public records; and acts done under statutory authority. These are similar to exceptions under copyright. However, there is no library copying permission which applies to database right covering extraction/reutilization for research or private study. So, even though non-electronic (printed) databases such as directories and encyclopaedias are purchased alongside other materials, they must now be treated differently. Exactly how this will work in practice is not known.

6 Future changes to the Act

Copyright Directive

This Proposal for a Directive on Harmonization of certain aspects of Copyright and Related Rights in the Information Society (COM(97)628 final) covers both the obligations in the WIPO treaties (see page 7) and the European Commission's plan to harmonize private copying. Despite the objective by the EC to harmonize the exceptions, all but one are left as options for the member states to include or not in national implementation. If member states opt to include them, then they have to abide by the exact conditions. There is no guarantee that any Member State will take up the options. Therefore they would not only be entirely unharmonized but also without any guarantee that they will be implemented to preserve a fair balance in copyright. All the exceptions given are also subject to the so-called three-step test – only for

> ... certain specific cases and shall not be interpreted in such a way as to allow their application to be used in a manner which unreasonably prejudices the rightholders' legitimate interests or conflicts with normal exploitation of their works or other subject matter.

When the Directive is adopted by the European Council, if the legitimate interests of librarians and consumers continue to be disregarded, it is likely that there will be radical changes introduced which will have to be implemented into UK copyright legislation. The 47 exceptions in the UK will be drastically reduced. At the time of writing (February 1999), these are the likely changes:

1 The UK will be forced to install levies for private copying, including copying under 'fair dealing' and for off-air recording at home. The Government has said that it is not in favour of levies.
2 A distinction will have to be made between analogue and digital copying. In the digital environment, any statutory provision given for copying will be for personal private use and be subject to a remuneration paid to rights holders.
3 The library regulations will be severely curtailed, as only certain not-for-profit libraries will be allowed to copy and then only for specific acts of reproduction made for documentation and conservation purposes only. This has been translated to mean archiving. There will be no copying for users (including document delivery) or for stock. Industrial and commercial libraries, and others which do not fit the narrow exception, will have to pay every time or be licensed for all copying.

4 The exception for education will have to be changed to reflect the current wording, which only allows for 'illustration for teaching or scientific research' provided it is of a non-commercial purpose and a remuneration is paid.

5 Technical protections may not be overridden. There is no provision given for circumventing a technical protection even for a lawful use. Also if a technical protection is applied to the work, any exception would be overridden and cease to apply.

6 Provision will have to be given for copying by people with disabilities, but this is likely to be negated by tape and equipment levies.

The earliest that changes will be introduced will be 2001. It is advised to follow details of the progress of this controversial Directive in the *LA record* or on the LA web pages, or on the EBLIDA website. (See also **Working for the profession** on page 52.)

7 Guidance on copying limits

Published literary works

Periodicals

Librarians of non-profit-based libraries are restricted to copying only one article from any periodical issue for their users [**S.38(1)**]. Accordingly, The Library Association recommends that users making their own copies (under fair dealing for research or private study) should not exceed the same limit.

An article is defined as 'any item'. When several small items appear together (e.g. news items without separate authors), they may be treated as one item unless they form an unreasonable proportion of the periodical issue. For example, it would be unreasonable to expect a user to ensure that a copy was not made of several unwanted items printed on an A4 page alongside the item one required. A contents page may count as one item (see **Contents pages** on page 55).

Official Journal of the EU

A generous attitude is adopted towards copying from the Official Journal as, similar to copying from Crown and Parliamentary material, it is in the EU's interest to disseminate the information contained therein. However, when photocopying it is advisable to stick to fair dealing amounts, as the generous attitude does not extend to the typographical arrangement. There is no limitation to the number of items allowed to be copied from any individual issue of the OJ if they are rekeyed, but the inclusion of photocopies of OJ texts requires permission in writing from the Office for Official Publications of the European Communities. For those with a CLA licence, the OJ is covered by the CLA licence repertoire.

Books

No statutory guidance is given for copying under fair dealing for research or private study, but the library regulations state that 'a reasonable proportion' may be copied. Although this has not been tested, it is generally agreed that one complete chapter, or a maximum otherwise of 5% of extracts, from a published work would be reasonable. This also follows the amount allowed to be copied under a CLA licence. Remember also that there are at least two copyrights in a book: the author's text and the publisher's typographical arrangement. If an author is out of copyright and the work was published over 25 years ago, then substantial parts of the text may be copied.

Short books, reports or pamphlets without chapters

The Library Association recommends that up to 10% of a work is reasonable for short works provided that the extract does not amount to more than 20 pages.

Poems, short stories and other short literary works

These are whole works in themselves and therefore should not be copied without permission, but when a collection or anthology, a short story or poem of not more than 10 pages may be copied. Remember also that a poem or short story whose author is out of copyright, contained in a collection or anthology published over 25 years ago, may be copied freely as the typographical arrangement copyright will also have expired. Poems embedded in a chapter of a book may be treated as part of the chapter.

British Standards

The BSI has agreed that up to 10% of a Standard may be copied. This amount is the same for copying from a printed Standard, microform or CD-ROM.

Crown and Parliamentary publications including HMSO material

In September 1996, HMSO published a fourth in the series of 'Dear Librarian' letters outlining what may be copied from Crown and Parliamentary copyright publications without further permission being sought. A copy of this letter is available from HMSO, and is also available on the web (**www.hmso.gov.uk/liblet.htm**). This latest letter reflects some of the changes arising out of HMSO privatization. The objective of the Copyright Unit at HMSO is to 'facilitate the widest possible dissemination of official material, while ensuring that all reproduction is proper and appropriate in the general public interest.' For copying above the extents and permissions outlined below, contact the Copyright Unit of HMSO. At the time of writing, HMSO has just published a White Paper on the future management of Crown Copyright, which may have a bearing on the following allowances:

1   It is permitted without formal permission or charge to copy the text from any single title or document from the list below in its entirety provided that
    - no more than one photocopy is made for any one individual
    - copies are not distributed to other individuals or organizations
    An exception is given to schools and places of higher education, where a single copy may be provided for each student.

2 It is permitted without formal permission or charge to make multiple photocopies of extracts from any title or document, provided that the extracts from any single work should not exceed 30% or one complete chapter or equivalent, whichever is the greater:

- Lords and Commons Official Reports (Hansard), Bills of Parliament, and House Business Papers, including Journals of both Houses, Lords Minutes, the Vote Bundle, Commons Order-Books, the Commons Public Bill Lists and Statutory Instruments Lists, the Weekly Information Bulletin and the Sessional Information Digest, all of which are Parliamentary copyright
- other Parliamentary papers published by HMSO, including Command Papers and Reports of Select Committees of both Houses
- Acts of Parliament, Statutory Instruments and Statutory Rules and Orders, which are Crown copyright
- press releases from departments, agencies or other Crown bodies (while these are obviously for unrestricted use at time of issue, they may be freely reproduced thereafter).

For other Crown and Parliamentary copyright texts, copying should be restricted to the recommended limits for research or private study in respect of books, pamphlets and reports. Photocopying is **not** allowed in connection with advertising or endorsement, or in circumstances which may be 'potentially libellous or slanderous of individuals, companies or organizations'. This is particularly relevant to Parliamentary material 'whose use must not give rise to unfair or misleading selection or undignified association'. It is also pointed out that Hansard enjoys special protection from proceedings for defamation. Anyone publishing non-official copies of proceedings in Parliament would not enjoy this protection.

Since 1997, the full text of Statutory Instruments is also published on the HMSO web pages. Individuals are authorized to download the text to a file or printer for their own individual use. HMSO also allows the reproduction of the text for the purpose of developing value-added products without prior permission or charge, provided that the reproduction is accurate, not malicious and is acknowledged as Crown copyright. Reproduction outside these terms requires the consent of the Copyright Unit at HMSO. Details are also included in the other HMSO letter 'Dear Publisher'.

Directories and other printed compilations

Directories and other compilations of data or works are non-electronic databases and are subject to the new database regulations (see page 25). Although there has not been any agreement with rights holders regarding safe amounts to copy, there can be no challenge if copying is limited to insubstantial (fair dealing) extracts for research or private study, provided, of course, that these do not add up to a substantial amount. Lawful users are also allowed to extract but not reutilize a substantial amount for the purposes of illustration for teaching or research. However, exactly what this means in practice is not known. It is advised that discretion is used if using this exception.

Yellow Pages

Yellow Pages is an example of a database which is protected by copyright and database right. BT, which owns the rights in the Yellow Pages directories, has confirmed that under fair dealing for research or private study purposes, one classified section may be copied provided that it is no more than five pages. Library users may therefore copy this amount for themselves. If a librarian does the copying for the user, then more may be copied. The LA recommends that copying should not be more than 5% and that users should sign a copyright declaration form. Users needing to copy more than 5% or for commercial purposes should be advised to contact BT for permission. BT are also able to supply business mailing lists.

Artistic works

Although artistic works may not be copied under the library regulations, copying under fair dealing is allowed although, like all fair dealing, it may be subject to a challenge of 'fairness'. Normally, copying whole works should only be done if permission or licence has been granted. **NB** Artistic works may be displayed or exhibited without permission because this does not infringe copyright.

Illustrations

These may be photocopied if they illustrate or form part of an article from a periodical, or are included in extracts from other material. Discretion should be used when copying them on their own since they may be complete works in themselves. It may be acceptable for pupils to copy an illustration for project work under fair dealing for research or private study, as long as no further copies are made without permission or licence. Following the agreement between DACS and the CLA, this will be covered by the CLA licence in due course.

Ordnance Survey maps

Even though librarians are not given statutory permission to copy artistic works under the library regulations, Ordnance Survey signed an agreement in 1993 with The Library Association, Joint Consultative Committee and the British Committee for Map Information and Cataloguing Systems (BRICMICS) to allow librarians to copy OS maps for their users subject to certain conditions. Requests must be accompanied by a copyright declaration form and meet the other conditions specified in the library regulations. The maximum amount which may be copied is four copies of a single extract from an Ordnance Survey or OS-based map not exceeding 625 sq cms (A4 size). These must be straight scale copies, i.e. they may not be enlarged. The same amount may be copied by individuals copying for themselves under fair dealing for the purposes of research or private study. This extends to making copies from digital mapping as well. The above agreement has now expired and negotiations are taking place to renew it. (See also **Ordnance Survey education licences**, page 42.)

Goad plans

Chas E. Goad supply their retail plans to public libraries with a licence to copy. Permission is given to copy for students only, provided evidence is given as proof, such as a student card or other acceptable form of identification, e.g. a school letterhead confirming their attendance at that establishment. It is advised that schools should make this arrangement and the conditions known to their students. The amount allowed to be copied is the same as from an OS map – up to four copies of a single extract not exceeding A4 (625 sq cms). Students will be required to sign a form declaring that the copy is for research or private study purposes only.

Photographs

Photographs, unlike literary or musical works, do not easily conform to the extract, proportional copying or quotation rules since, in many instances and especially in the case of vertical aerial photographs, even a segment from an original photograph can produce an image which is considered a complete work in itself. This indivisibility of visual materials has led to the situation where it is generally acceptable to rights holders for complete photographs to be copied in the following circumstances: under fair dealing for research or private study; when the copy is of a lesser resolution quality than the original; when the image is defaced or clearly marked in some way; or the characteristics of the copied image clearly indicate that it is a derivative and not a first-generation item from the creator's original work. Whatever the resolution quality of the copy, individuals may make copies of photographs for their own private and domestic use. Individuals may make copies of photographs provided the rights holder has not prohibited copying of the work.

Slides or transparencies

One slide or transparency, but not from photographic works, may be made to accompany a lecture provided that the slide or transparency cannot be purchased from a commercial source. However, such copies may not be deposited as part of a collection in the library. The Design and Artists Copyright Society has said that copying of artistic works by students onto slides for project work falls under fair dealing as long as subsequent reproductions are not made without permission. Making transparencies from illustrations, photographs or plates in books or other published works for library collections is almost certainly likely to infringe the Act. Unless licensed to do so (see **DACS slide licensing scheme** on page 39), it is advisable to include in slide collections only: transparencies purchased from a commercial source, those made with the permission of the rights holder, and those made from sources which are out of copyright.

Printed music

The fair dealing exception for copying for research or private study applies to printed music. Librarians may also make and supply a copy of a part of a musical work under the library regulations. Copyright in printed music may be held by more than one person or body. It is advised that short extracts only should be copied for research or private study. Making multiple copies of music without permission would be an infringement. The Code of Fair Practice agreed between composers and publishers of printed music states that

> . . . bona fide students or teachers, whether they are in an educational establishment or not may, without application to the copyright owner, make copies of short excerpts of musical works provided that they are for study only (not for performance). Copying whole movements or whole works is expressly forbidden under this permission.

This booklet also outlines other permissions to copy for specific circumstances. See the *Code of fair practice for printed music* (revised edition) Music Publishers' Association. See also **Visually impaired persons** on page 64.

8 Licensing schemes

The UK Act encourages the use of the law of contract for collective licensing. Licensing 'schemes' must cover works of more than one author. Contracts such as licences are a matter for agreement between parties, normally outside legislation. Contract law can override copyright law, so it is important that no contract or licence negates what one may do under statute. On the contrary, a licence should give more user rights to copy and use. An important feature of the Act is the establishment of a Copyright Tribunal to arbitrate on the terms and conditions of licensing schemes. As yet, it has not been convened to arbitrate in any licensing scheme affecting the library and information or teaching professions.

Copyright Licensing Agency licensing schemes

The Copyright Licensing Agency (CLA) is the main licensing body for reprographic copying from most UK books and periodicals. The CLA acts mainly as agent for the Authors' Licensing and Collecting Society and the Publishers' Licensing Society. Most LEA schools and colleges of further education, all universities and institutes of higher education, many schools and colleges in the independent sector, some Government departments, some industry sectors and commercial companies are licensed by the Copyright Licensing Agency to make multiple copies within clearly defined limits from most books, journals and periodicals for specific purposes. The CLA distributes monies collected from licences to authors and publishers as compensation for the copying of their works. This is mainly based on a system of sampling among institutions or user surveys. Licensees, provided they do not breach the conditions of the licence, are indemnified against prosecution from authors and publishers covered by their repertoire. It is advisable for library managers to examine the licence and/or the Good Practice Guidelines issued by the CLA in order to take note of all the conditions. Licences should be kept by designated Licensing Coordinators.

Although the CLA has a mandate to include most books and journals, it has a large list of excluded categories and works, which should always be checked before copying. The list may be examined on the CLA website. This does not always mean that these works may not be copied. Some works may be covered by another licence, e.g. newspapers. An excluded work or category may also mean that the copyright owner will allow copying a greater extent than under fair dealing or the library regulations. **NB** When no licence is available, teachers may copy for instruction purposes 1% of material in any quarterly period (see **Copying for instruction** on page 19).The CLA has now signed an Artistic Works Licence agreement with DACS to allow photocopying of artistic works from published material. It will be offered first to the higher education sector in 1999.

CLA licence for LEA schools (England and Wales)

The terms and conditions of the latest basic licence for schools remain largely unchanged. The extent of copying from books and journals is still up to one chapter or 5% of a book, an entire short story or poem not exceeding ten pages in length, or the whole or part of one article from a journal or periodical issue. Copies may only be made on the licensed premises and the

> ... number of multiple copies of any one item of copyright material made for any one course of study or for a lesson or other formal instruction or study within that course or for a meeting of parents, teachers or governors shall not exceed the number needed to ensure that each pupil and their teacher or each parent, teacher or governor has one copy each.

The notable difference in the new agreement is that the limitation on the number of copies per pupil per year has been raised from 20 copies per pupil per year to 100 copies per pupil per year. Also there is no longer a requirement under the new terms for schools to keep log books in order to monitor the number of copies being made per pupil.

No electronic storage of licensed material may be made (apart from faxed copies). Only reproductions on paper may are allowed.

Provided there is no large-print version available, permission is also given in the licence to make enlarged copies (minimum16-point type size) of up to the whole of a book, journal or periodical for the use by partially sighted pupils and staff only (see **Visually impaired persons** on page 64).

Schools will be selected on a sampling basis for the CLA Record Keeping Scheme to establish what and how much is copied, in order to calculate what should be reimbursed to rights holders.

CLA licensing scheme for Education and Library Boards (Northern Ireland)

This licensing scheme is virtually the same as that for England and Wales, except that there is no limit on the number of copies which may be made per pupil per year.

CLA licence for LEA schools (Scotland)

The original agreement expired in 1997 but has been extended annually on the same conditions. The scheme is in two parts: Part A allows up to 20 copies per pupil per year, which can be apportioned differently by LEAs between schools; Part B allows further copying subject to an agreed price per copy. If both bands have been bought, this allows further copies to be made per pupil per year subject to the appropriate payment. The copying conditions of the Scottish licence are similar to those of other LEAs

> The number of multiple copies of any one item of copyright material made for any one course of study or for a lesson or other formal instruction or study within that course or for a meeting of parents, teachers or governors shall not exceed the number needed to ensure that each pupil and their teacher or each parent, teacher or governor has one copy each.

Copies may only be made on the licensed premises. The extent of copying from books and journals is: up to one chapter or 5% of a book; an entire short story or poem not exceeding ten pages in length; the whole or part of one article from a journal or periodical issue. Schools also have to submit record-keeping forms to the CLA on a regular basis to include details of items copied.

Although it is not yet part of the licensing scheme, Scottish schools may take advantage of the protocol to allow copying for partially sighted students and staff.

At the time of writing (February 1999) the CLA is in negotiation with COSLA about one licensing scheme for schools and local authorities, which is likely to be similar to that for the other LEAs.

Independent sector and resource centres

The CLA has devised similar licensing schemes for schools in the independent sector, and in local authorities in the Channel Islands. The vast majority of resource centres are included within the LEA schools scheme. Please contact the CLA for details.

British Library/CLA Agreement

The British Library Document Supply Centre (BLDSC) has a licensing agreement with the CLA to provide a copyright-cleared service. This licence allows the supply of copyright material to libraries over and above the limitations of the library regulations, and so removes the conditions of supply, permits longer extracts and more copies, and more than one extract from the same issue of a journal. The BL states that the copies supplied may only be copied further if it is allowed under statute or licence.

DACS slide licensing scheme

The problem of not being legally authorized to make slides of copies of artistic works in published editions, and to build up a collection of such slides for use in education, has been addressed by the Design and Artists' Copyright Society. DACS is the collecting society representing the interests of visual artists, including commercial artists and photographers. With the guidance of a steering group of user representatives, DACS has developed a blanket slide licensing scheme. The scheme is in two parts: an agreement to declare and pay for any existing collection; and an annual licence for making new slides.

Organizations with an existing collection, including any illegally produced slides, are required to declare the approximate number and pay a fee. This is a one-off payment to DACS, which is calculated according to the size of the collection. In return for payment and compliance with the terms of the agreement, DACS indemnifies the institution against claims of copyright infringement by artists for their works held in collections.

The annual licence permits establishments to produce new and add existing slides to the collection. A flat-rate fee is payable for the first year, and subsequent annual payments are calculated on the number of slides added to the collection during each year.

The licensing scheme for slide collections permits the reproduction of up to ten copies for educational purposes of artistic works onto slides, acetates or transparencies, and these may be stored in the library. Included in the definition of artistic works are: paintings, sculptures, collages, engravings or prints, drawings, photographs, other graphic works and works of artistic craftsmanship. It does not cover film stills, advertisements, mapping or trade marks. DACS may be contacted for further guidance on the scheme.

Off-air recording licensing schemes

Two licensing schemes are available for recording radio and television programmes for educational purposes: the licensing scheme from the Educational Recording Agency (ERA) to cover all terrestrial broadcasting with the exception of Open University programmes, and the Open University Educational Enterprises (OUEE) licensing scheme, which covers Open University programmes. Any off-air recording of terrestrial channels must be covered by one or other of these schemes. Satellite and cable channels are, at the time of writing, not covered by licences. Until they are, off-air recording for educational purposes is free.

ERA licence

The ERA licence is restricted to educational establishments only. This has been clarified to include all institutions, however funded, which provide further education as defined in subsection 2 (S.41) of the Education Act 1944 as amended by the Education Reform Act 1988. Payment for this licence is according to the number of pupils in the school. Once licensed, schools may designate individuals to make off-air recordings of radio and television programmes both in the school and from home. Within the conditions of the licence, tapes may be copied further, used in class, catalogued and kept indefinitely in library collections and loaned to students. Licensed schools may also borrow and copy recordings belonging to other ERA licence holders. Refer to ERA for a copy of their useful little guide to the scheme.

OUEE licence

This scheme works differently from ERA. Payment depends on the total number of recordings which are kept for longer than 30 days. OUEE requires each recording to be registered. Each establishment then has 30 days in which to view and delete the recording to avoid having to pay. No loans for use off the premises are permitted.

British Standards Institution licence

This licence allows multiple copying for class purposes. Special bulk discounts are available when whole documents are needed. Otherwise the licence permits copying of substantial portions of standard specifications, short of whole documents. Details from the British Standards Institution.

Newspaper Licensing Agency

The NLA scheme was launched in 1996 to enable the copying of works in its repertoire for internal management purposes and for ad hoc copying. Licensees, provided they do not breach the conditions of the licence, are indemnified against prosecution. The scheme is aimed mainly at commercial organizations and cuttings agencies, but educational establishments, government departments, professional organizations, and the public and voluntary sector, are also entitled to be licensed if they make copies from the newspapers covered by the licence over and above the copying limits for research or private study. The scheme covers all the UK national and 31 Scottish and regional newspapers. Some local newspapers now belong to the scheme. The *Times Educational* and the *Times Higher* supplements are not covered by the scheme.

The fees charged are based on the type of licence and vary according to the type of organization. Schools whose pupils are aged 16 and below are able to obtain a free licence from the NLA. The licence covers photocopying from the NLA repertoire up to 250 copies from any one article for internal management purposes (including instruction). Like the CLA licence, it does not cover artistic works. If an institution wishes to copy and store for dissemination electronically, permission must be obtained from the individual newspaper publisher concerned.

Schools and resource centres wishing to make multiple copies from the above newspapers should obtain a licence. Full details are available from the NLA.

Ordnance Survey licences

LEA schools may copy for educational purposes under the Local Authority licence from OS mapping which has been legitimately obtained. This may be done on the premises or by an outside contracted printer.

Schools may also obtain copies from the OS mapping held in the public library under this licence. There is no size restriction when supplying large scale maps (i.e. 1:10000, 1:2500 or 1:1250 scales). However, at small scales (1:25000 and smaller) copies must not exceed A4 size. It is advisable to contact the public library in advance in order to make it clear that the copying is for educational purposes under the terms of the licence. Otherwise, public libraries are obliged to limit the copying to fair dealing amounts. If the copying is for a purpose other than educational, e.g. copying for inclusion in a prospectus, then an extra licence for business must be obtained from OS.

Christian Copyright Licensing International

The CCLI is part of a worldwide network linking authors, copyright owners and publishers. It licenses the copying of the lyrics of hymns, songs of worship and children's songs which are in copyright. This material is excluded from the CLA licence. The Music Reproduction Licence allows the making of multiple copies from hymn and worship song books which have been purchased by the licensee. CCLI licenses schools as well as churches and Christian organizations to copy from their repertoire. It is not comprehensive, but CCLI state that they cover the words and music of over 120,000 hymns and songs which are in copyright. Costs for the full 'words and music' licence are based on student numbers, and range from £51 for up to 49 students to £384 for up to 2,999 students. A 'words only' licence is cheaper.

9 Copyright of works in electronic form

The exclusive right of reproduction given to authors includes storing the work in electronic form. The contents of works which are 'published' in electronic format, such as material on CD-ROMs, online databases, floppy disks etc., are thus protected in the same way as their printed equivalents. Any kind of electronic copying or transmitting which involves storage of a copyright-protected work is part of the restricted right of reproduction. Even storage which is of a transient or incidental nature, e.g. a cache copy, is regarded as a reproduction.

Problems of access

Because works in electronic form are very easy to copy, rights holders are even more vociferous about protecting their works from misuse and abuse, as well as not wishing to lose money on their economic investment. Their main concern is piracy. Many rights holders are therefore reluctant to allow their works to be stored in digital form, as it is difficult and sometimes impossible to control or detect the movement of works electronically. Once digitized and stored in a computer, works can be transferred unseen. An author or a publisher will be reluctant to give *carte blanche* permission for a work to be available electronically without some guarantee that it will not be misused and abused, or sent around the network to countries where copyright protection is inadequate. Another concern is the potential for the violation of an author's moral rights. Works can be manipulated easily while in electronic format, which infringes the author's right of integrity and increases the risk of plagiarism.

Technical solutions

Technical solutions – electronic copyright management systems (ECMS) – may be an answer, provided these will not negate a statutory exception if one exists (see **EU Copyright Directive** on page 29). Much research is going into looking for effective technical solutions – such as encryption, tagging, digital fingerprinting, digital object identifiers (DOI), watermarking etc. – which will add extra protection to back up copyright. Depending on their sophistication, these will be able to track and control the movement of works in digital form. Used effectively, some will also be used to authenticate content and provide information on the status of the intellectual property as well as prevent unauthorized access. Although much of what will be protected will be entertainment

e products, there is a danger that some devices, designed to prevent copyright
___, __ _ld also be used to control access and demand high prices. The LA along with
other user groups is concerned that there should be an effective balance between controls and access for legitimate users (see **Lobbying activities** on page 52).

Contractual solutions and digital licensing initiatives

In the meantime, most library uses of works in electronic form will need to have the permission or licence of rights holders. Librarians have to gain new skills in negotiating deals
with publishers. This problem is not unique to the UK. It is an international issue.
Various discussions have been taking place between groups of publishers and the library
and information sector. Some publishers are beginning to understand that resource
sharing between libraries is not prejudicing their economic interests. Below is a selection of some of the major licensing initiatives.

Consortium licensing – ICOLC

The growth of bilateral agreements between publishers and librarians has led to a mul-
tiplicity of complex and varied conditions, not all of which are easily comprehended or
digested by busy library staff. Some librarians had better deals than others. Many were
more concerned with their budgets than worrying about what a licence allowed. It was
realized by some librarians that they could be in a better position to improve these deals
with publishers if they pooled information and knowledge, and so library consortia were
born. Consortium licensing is being seen by many, mainly academic, librarians to be the
answer to the might of publishers. Now many national consortium groups have joined
forces to share licensing information and to produce a set of licensing principles.
Together with other 80 other consortia world-wide, the International Coalition of
Library Consortia (ICOLC) was formed. In March 1998, ICOLC published a
Statement of Current Perspective and Preferred Practices for the Selection and Purchase
of Electronic Information (**www.library.yale.edu/consortia/statement.html**).

ECUP

ECUP with its successor ECUP+ is a concerted action supported by EBLIDA and
funded by the European Commission (DGX111). The EU project was completed in
January 1999 but its sister project CECUP continues in Eastern and Central Europe
until 2000. The aims of ECUP were to raise awareness and stimulate discussions on
copyright issues, and to devise model licensing clauses for the use of electronic information. ECUP produced some useful documents, two of which were matrices: one on
digitization and use of print-based library material in copyright; and the other on use of
commercially published digital works. Access to these works was dependent on the

library sector, the type of user and whether access was on or off site.

Based on the ECUP matrices, discussions took place between EBLIDA, ECUP and STM, which resulted in a consensus on digital archiving and electronic usage by libraries of STM print journals. A joint statement outlining a set of principles was issued in November 1998. (EBLIDA/ECUP/STM Joint statement on incidental digitization and storage of STM print journal articles). Also, ECUP has published a set of guiding principles (*How to avoid licensing pitfalls*) to help librarians understand the legal consequences of certain clauses in a licence when negotiating licences. (**www.eblida.org**).

NESLI [www.nesli.ac.uk]

NESLI, the National Electronic Site Licensing Initiative, is an organization which aims to perform four basic functions: to provide a negotiating body to represent the UK higher education sector in discussion with primary publishers; to handle the transactions (subscriptions) arising from any successfully negotiated arrangements; to provide a single interface for accessing the electronic journals included in the initiative; to explore and implement a range of additional, value-added services; and to contribute to the resolution of some of the barriers preventing a more rapid take-up of electronic journals. A NESLI Model Licence has been developed by the NESLI Steering Group, and represents the interests of both publishers and the library community. The NESLI Steering Group, working closely with the Publishers Association/Joint Information Systems Committee Licensing Working Group, aims to promote the convergence between the NESLI and JISC/PA licences.

CLA digitization licence

Following a requirements gathering exercise in May 1998, the CLA is proposing to licence digitization of materials. The licence is likely to be transactional, not a blanket licence like the photocopy model, to be managed by CLARCS, and only to include works for which the CLA has a positive mandate. The fees will be determined by rights holders themselves. Once cleared for digitization, a work will only be accessed by designated employees. The digitized works can be made available online including to distance learning students. The works may also be printed off, photocopied and distributed. The licence will be offered first to the higher education sector and some parts of the commercial and industrial sector.

Fair dealing, the library regulations and digital works

The question is, do the exceptions still apply? There is nothing in the Act to say that the exceptions (fair dealing and the library regulations etc.) do not apply to works in digital form, so it is assumed that copying of a digital work is allowed within limits. What one has to weigh up, given the concerns of rights holders, is what are the safe limits of fair dealing? What are the risks of prosecution? In the HE sector there have been wide discussions with publishers on what constitutes fair dealing in using and copying electronic products in text form. Their subsequent report contains a very useful set of common-sense fair dealing guidelines (**www.ukoln.ac/services/elib/papers/pa/**). For instance, copying part of an electronic publication onto paper by an individual. or by a librarian for that individual. is considered to be fair dealing. Similarly copying part of an electronic publication onto disk (portable or fixed medium) for permanent local electronic storage by an individual for research or private study purposes is also fair dealing.

The problem with copying under the library regulations is that a request cannot be received by e-mail. Copyright declaration forms have to be completed and signed by the requester. and UK law does not (at present) recognize electronic signatures. So electronic requests are limited to fax. Once all the conditions have been fulfilled, librarians may copy for their users from a digital work. The EU has a directive in the pipeline on digital signatures: Proposal for a European Parliament and Council Directive on a common framework for electronic signatures COM(1998)297/2 which is likely to streamline electronic requests.

10 Guidance on digital copying

Rekeying from paper format into a word processor

It is advised that whole works, or substantial portions of works, should not be rekeyed without permission. It is acceptable to rekey extracts from copyright-protected material under fair dealing, e.g. for criticism or review (provided due acknowledgement is given).

Downloading from commercial databases

Downloading from an online database is usually permitted only under the terms of the licence from the database owner as part of the service contract. How much one is allowed to download depends on the contract with the database provider, so it is essential for subscribers to study any contracts for limitations on downloading (copying). However, the new regulations regarding databases give some basic access rights for using databases protected by database right: lawful users of a database are authorized to do anything necessary to enable them to access and use the contents. It is also stated that, even if there is a term or condition in any contract which accompanies such a database which purports to prohibit or restrict this lawful use, this can be ignored. A lawful user is also allowed to extract or reutilize *insubstantial* parts of a database which has been made available to the public in any manner, and any term or condition in any agreement to use such a database which prevents such extraction or reutilization shall be void. Lawful users are also allowed to extract, but not reutilize, substantial parts for the purposes of illustration for teaching or research, provided it is non-commercial. Reutilization covers all forms of making contents available, whether in print or electronic fixed media, online transmission, or broadcasting etc., so extracting is likely to mean merely displaying on screen.

The supply of a CD-ROM is determined by a contract of purchase (conditions of sale) if it is bought outright, or if it is leased, a leasing contract. It is advisable, however, to check the subscription contracts, or conditions of purchase or supply, to determine exactly what is permissible. However, fair dealing still applies to copyright-protected databases provided copying is not for commercial research. Under database right, lawful users are authorized to access and use the contents, and to download insubstantial parts regardless of the contract. A lawful user is also allowed to extract or reutilize *insubstantial* parts of a database which has been made available to the public in any manner, and any term or condition in any agreement to use such a database which prevents such extraction or reutilization shall be void. Lawful users are also allowed to extract, but not reutilize, substantial parts for the purposes of illustration for teaching or research provided it is non-commercial. Any other copying and using, such as downloading to disk or delivering digitally, needs to be explicitly allowed in the contract.

Sending copyright works by fax

Although fax is a common form of communication, copying a copyright work and sending it by fax is a legal grey area. Faxing a copy of copyright material – for example, a journal article – means (a) storing it in an electronic form, and (b) making an extra hard copy to use in the machine. These are 'transient or incidental to some other use of the work' [S.17(2) & (6)] and thus could be seen to be infringing copyright. However, as long as the fax transmission is performed under a legitimate copyright exception, there should be no infringement. Even if the electronic copy falls under the reproduction right (see **EU Directive on Harmonization of Copyright and Related Rights in the Information Society** on page 29) this type of transient copying for a legitimate purpose is likely to be exempted. The LA advises that if the transmitted hard copy is destroyed, and all the relevant copyright regulations have been complied with (the signed declaration has been obtained before copying), there should be no problem.

However, with the increasing sophistication of this equipment – fax modems and photocopiers with fax facilities – the recipient is often able to receive the copy in electronic form, which implies storage. This could be challenged by as an infringing act. Therefore it is advised that, unless permission has been obtained from rights holders, senders and recipients should delete the electronic version as soon as a single copy has been printed by the recipient.

E-mail messages and discussion lists

Many assume that e-mail recipients may use messages freely. However, the copyright in e-mails, like letters, belongs to the author (or the employer if they are created as part of the employment contract). Permission to copy and use is often implied and understood, so to keep e-mails personal and confidential, a notice to that effect should be included in the message. Sending a message to a public discussion list is like sending a letter to the editor of a newsletter, i.e. an implied licence is given to share the contents with subscribers unless there was clear evidence to the contrary. The copyright in the message still belongs to the sender, even though it may be forwarded to other lists, quoted and archived. Moral rights also apply, so a message should never be quoted without being acknowledged; it should not be attributed to someone else; nor should it be manipulated or treated in a derogatory fashion. Messages sent to a closed list should not be forwarded to a public list without the sender's permission being sought. All copyright notices attached to e-mails should be respected.

Using digital scanners

Although the potential for storage and preservation of paper-based library materials is enormous, the legality of scanning of copyright-protected works (other than those belonging to the school or resource centre) in order to preserve them is unclear, and it is recommended that until the situation is clarified, permission should be sought for this practice. For fair dealing purposes, scanning an article or an insubstantial part of a work *may* be acceptable. For example, as long as the work was acknowledged, a student could scan an extract of a work onto their own personal computer for project or coursework purposes. It may not be fair dealing subsequently to use the work in a commercial publication without clearance, so if a student wished to publish a work, the inclusion of any extracts (other than any short extracts quoted for criticism or review) may have to be cleared. It would also be unfair dealing to scan a work to place it on the web, or to make further copies and circulate them to others. The scanning and experimental manipulation of images is also fraught with difficulty, as an artist's moral rights are involved. Again, if an image stays on a personal computer, this *may* not be high-risk. Schools should use their discretion and maybe devise a policy on whether to allow such practices. If scanning onto a communal hard disk, it is advisable to wipe it clean it periodically in case anything has been inadvertently stored. It is also advisable to place copyright warning notices by any copying equipment (see **Posters** on page 75).

Internet and the World Wide Web

Provided they meet the criteria for protection, works which appear on the Internet are someone's intellectual property. Many believe that material on the Internet is copyright-free. This is not so. All the rules of copyright which apply to printed material also apply to works in digital form. Collections of documents on websites are clearly databases and all the rules regarding databases apply. What appears sometimes to be free from copyright restrictions may just be copyright-waived. Some works have notices to this effect (see example below). At present much of the content on the Internet is there for the express purpose of its being read, copied or downloaded. Some of it is ephemeral. Some material may even consist of infringing copies. It is difficult for some content providers to control copying and reuse of their material, but if material is difficult to access and copy – for example, accessed via a password – it is clear that such content providers are not waiving their copyright and so conditions of use should be respected. Similarly, reading conditions of access on screen, and clicking to say that these are understood and accepted, means one has entered into a form of contract. The option is always there of negotiating with content providers for uses over and above these terms. It is generally accepted that, if no explicit copyright notice is attached to the material, there is an implicit licence to copy. Discretion should be used, of course, especially with commercial reuse and if in doubt users should be encouraged to stick to the generally agreed fair dealing amounts for copying from printed works. If there is a helpful notice on material which allows more copying and use than (normally allowed) under statute, then copying may take place within these limits .

Uploading copyright-protected works onto the Internet, whether to a web page or as part of an electronic mail message, is storing the works in electronic form, which is a restricted act and should not normally be done without permission or licence.

Creating webpages and intranets

Copying for a workplace intranet should not be done without first obtaining clearance from the owners of the relevant websites. Any content place on a website should either be owned entirely by the school or be cleared by obtaining permission to use. The copyright in the actual website (which is in effect a database), regardless of content, is owned by its maker. Although the copyright holder is entitled to prevent unauthorized copying from the site, in practice this may be difficult to control. At present, it would be foolish to put protected works on a website if one did not want them copied. In any case, recognizing the restricted copying allowed under a statutory exception is good public relations. It is suggested that a helpful copyright notice such as the one given in the example below should be placed on a website opening screen indicating what may be copied and for what purposes. Some basic points to note:

1   Make sure that all the content on a website has been cleared for inclusion.

Copyright in all contributions to this website remains with [the organization]. [The organization] holds exclusive rights in respect of electronic publication and dissemination. No part of this website may be posted or in any way mirrored on the WWW or any other part of the Internet without permission from [the organization]. No link should be made to this site without permission from [the organization].

Subject to this, permission is granted to download items for offline reading and use subject to the following conditions:

1   Print-outs should not be sold for profit purposes.
2   [The organization] name should remain attached to any copies.

Permission is granted to download articles, store them electronically on disk, and make multiple copies for [educational or personal] purposes subject to the following condition:

3   No charge should be made for access to users within the educational establishment.

Please contact [the organization] if necessary, for clarification of these terms or if you wish to use the material outside the permissions given above.

Fig. 10.1   *An example of a web copyright notice*

2 If the site is being developed by someone else, make sure that all the relevant authorizations (assignments or licences of copyright works) are obtained from the developer before the site goes live.

3 Ensure that any regular contributors are aware of the risks of website publication and the dangers of infringement, and obtain, preferably in writing, an agreement with all contributors to include assurances and indemnities to protect your organization against possible claims for copyright infringement.

Hypertext links

Since the judgement on the **Shetland Times** case (see **Case law** on page 73), it is not advisable to make any links to external websites which seek to bypass a homepage. Also, although not legally required, it is good practice to seek permission before linking, and to review such links on a regular basis in case they are no longer valid. Webmasters do not usually refuse permission.

11 Working for the profession – lobbying activities

LA/JCC Working Party on Copyright

This Working Party is a merger of the LA Sub-committee on Copyright and the Joint Consultative Committee's (JCC) Sub-committee on Copyright representing the members of the following organizations: Aslib: the Association for Information Management, the Institute of Information Scientists, The Library Association (representing all sectors), SCONUL (Standing Conference of National and University Libraries) and the Society of Archivists. Other organizations represented in the Working Party are: the British Library, the Royal National Institute for the Blind (RNIB), the Art Libraries Society of the UK and Ireland (ARLIS), and the International Association of Music Libraries, Archives and Documentation Centres (IAML) UK. The Working Party is the main voice speaking and lobbying on copyright on behalf of the library and information profession. It is concerned that the economic rights of creators and information providers are balanced with the needs of library and information staff and their users to gain access to information. As the voice of the profession on copyright, it frequently responds to Government and EU consultation documents. See the LA webpages for recent responses (**www.la-hq.org.uk**).

EFPICC

EFPICC – the European Fair Practices in Copyright Campaign – is an alliance of concerned European consumer groups, consumer electronics industries, education, library and disability groups to lobby for a sufficient level of access and affordable use of copyrighted information in a digital environment. EBLIDA (European Bureau of Library and Information Documentation Associations) represents European librarians on EFPICC. The LA is also a constituent part of EFPICC (UK). EFPICC members believe that adequate access to digital copyright works would be safeguarded by ensuring that certain fair practices apply to all types of libraries and archival institutions. The LA believes that such fair practices are more likely to lead to harmonization than the narrow EU proposals contained in the EU Copyright Directive, and that such uses should not be confused with illegal copying for commercial gain as is the case with piracy. Some of these fair practices are:

- viewing, browsing, listening to, and copying of, digital material for private, educational and research purposes in libraries and archives

- making a digital copy for archival and preservation purposes by libraries and archival institutions
- copying a limited number of pages on paper or on diskette of a digital work by libraries and archival institutions for their users
- making a copy on audio, visual or audio-visual recording media by private individuals for personal use and for non-commercial ends.

12 Miscellaneous advice and guidance

Charging for copying

There is no requirement to levy a charge when copying under the terms of a CLA licence. There is also no requirement under the Act to charge for copies under the fair dealing provisions. Staff or students making their own copies on self-operated photocopiers under those provisions will, in many libraries, pay the cost involved either by inserting money in the machine or by paying for a photocopying 'credit card'. Such charges are neither required nor prevented by the Act.

However, under the library regulations, librarians are required to charge the actual cost of making copies, plus a 'contribution to the general expenses of the library'. No advice can be given as to the meaning of a 'contribution to the general expenses of the library' since it is undefined. Libraries should, however, include a reasonable amount in the charges made to users over and above the direct costs, to cover handling costs. Photocopies obtained from other libraries may be paid for by the requesting library by using BL Document Supply Centre request forms as currency. Libraries have to make their own decisions about how they effect charging for the actual cost of making copies when they are obtained via interlibrary loan, as the Act offers no guidance on 'charging' users directly or recharging within the library budget margins.

Some libraries offering current awareness services have introduced the device of accepting money in advance from requesting institutions, and drawing from that deposit as requests are made. It is believed that this is an acceptable practice, although it cannot be regarded as authorized by the Act.

Committee papers

It seems clear that multiple copies required by a committee for consideration at a meeting would not be regarded as fair dealing for 'research'. 'Private study' is clearly not applicable in the case of committees. It has been argued that 'criticism or review' is an appropriate purpose for committees. Multiple copies are allowed for this fair dealing purpose. However, the intention was probably to allow quotations to be made from published works in reviews of those works published in newspapers and magazines (see **Fair dealing: criticism or review** on page 15). It also appears that permission can only apply to copying the text rather than the typographical layout. So photocopying an extract from a report would not be allowed, although retyping it *might* be. Similar considerations apply to fair dealing for current events.

On the other hand, it is in the interests of the publishers and copyright owners of many documents that other organizations should consider them and respond to them. This is especially so in the case of consultative documents. The following 'rules of thumb' are offered to assist in preparing committee papers:

1 **Circular letters and similar documents seeking the views of individuals and organizations**: it may be assumed that copies may be made without permission.
2 **Unpriced consultative documents**: if an unpriced document is labelled 'consultative' or similar, it may be assumed that the publisher wishes it to be widely circulated in order to receive comments. In most cases, it will probably be acceptable to copy it for committees. Free additional copies may be easily available from the publisher, in which case this may be the preferred option.
3 **Priced consultative documents**: it would be wise to obtain permission to copy either an extract or the whole document. An extract worth copying for a committee, e.g. the conclusions and recommendations, could be considered a 'substantial' part.
4 **Crown and Parliamentary publications:** see page 32.
5 **All other priced publications**: it is advisable to obtain permission from the publishers.

Many publishers will freely give permission to copy for committee purposes, if asked. All copies made for committee should have a full bibliographical reference, the source of 'official' copies, and should be marked 'for committee consideration only'. It cannot be assumed that committee members may make further copies to circulate in their workplace, for example. Unless specific permission has been obtained, it is advisable not to include copies of copyright documents with sets of committee papers which are sent to other people for information only. Sources of supply of the original documents may instead be included on agendas, or digests could be prepared.

Contents pages

The contents page of a journal could be counted as an article. Under the library regulations, only one article may be copied from a journal issue, and then only if it has been requested by a user. Therefore, copying and circulating contents pages could be seen as copyright infringement. However, it is the view of the LA that circulating journal contents pages is a way of advertising the journals and does not necessarily damage the economic rights of rights holders. In fact, the opposite damages economic rights: if users do not know what is in the journal, the journal is less likely to be read, and when budgets are tight these journals are more likely to be cancelled. There are some publishers who agree with our view and do not see this practice as encouraging copyright infringement, but other publishers disagree. Therefore, although the LA is unable to advise that making multiple copies of contents pages is free from the risk of prosecution, it is our view that it is unlikely that rights holders would object if a single copy of a journal contents page was displayed or circulated provided it was only to a specified group of users (see also **Current awareness bulletins** below).

Copyright-cleared workbooks

Some publishers allow the free copying of these workbooks. The price of copying is incorporated into the purchase price. However, copies should only be used by staff and students within the establishment, as it would be unfair to borrow a copy from another library or school resource centre to take advantage of the copyright-waived material.

Copying by students in public libraries

Many public libraries are used by students doing research for project work as they may be more convenient to use than academic libraries. The CLA licence does not extend to public libraries, and public librarians have to abide by the library regulations. The LA advises that, where necessary, public libraries and educational establishments should cooperate on the provision of photocopies of material for group projects. Students may still copy for research and private study under fair dealing.

Current awareness bulletins

Anyone may produce an in-house current awareness bulletin if the bibliographic details have been input manually, i.e. they have not been obtained by photocopying contents pages or downloaded from an online database. Own annotations may be included, and S.60 allows any abstracts published along with articles in scientific or technical journals to be incorporated in a current awareness bulletin, either by photocopying or rekeying, unless a licensing scheme becomes available to cover the copying of such abstracts (there is no licensing scheme at present for abstracts). The interpretation of 'scientific' or 'technical' may be assumed to be broad.

The Act clearly authorizes non-profit-based libraries to provide a copying service to any member of the public in response to requests. However, any library which advertised a copying service in direct association with a bulletin, especially if distributed beyond the normal clientele or catchment area, could be considered to be soliciting requests rather than responding to them. Such services could damage rights-owner markets because local demand for the original media concerned might be reduced if reliance is placed on current awareness and copying. Therefore, The Library Association recommends that any library sending bulletin copies outside its own clientele or catchment area should include the following statement:

> Those wishing to obtain copies of items in this issue should consult their own (or 'local') libraries.

It is also preferable to include standard declaration forms only in issues distributed to the library's own clientele. If forms are included in all copies, it should be made clear that they are for use only by registered members in the relevant catchment area or 'closed' clientele.

It is an infringement to make multiple copies of relevant journal articles as part of an SDI service and disseminate them to users. Contents pages are covered by copyright in the same way as other items in journals (see also **Contents pages** on page 55).

Damaged tapes

There is no provision in the Act for making back-up copies of commercially produced sound recordings or videos. A cassette tape damaged beyond repair which is still required for loan would have to be discarded and another purchased. If the material is no longer available for purchase, a copy may be made from another source (see **Copying for replacement** on page 18), but under this regulation the replacement copy has to be for reference only. The Mechanical Copyright Protection Society will license the copying of commercially produced sound recordings.

Declaration forms

Signed declaration forms should be kept by the library, which is making the copies as this would be part of the evidence if a case of alleged copyright infringement was brought against the library. For legislative purposes these forms should be kept for six years after the end of the year the copying took place, because an action under the legislation may be made at any time until six years after the alleged infringement occurred. There is nothing in the Act to suggest in what order they should be kept.

The Library Association has been advised that sending a photocopy declaration form by fax is acceptable. Where fax copies are on non-permanent paper, originals will still be needed for record keeping. Electronic signatures are at present not recognized under UK law. (See also **Fair dealing, the library regulations and digital works** on page 45.)

Exhibitions

Artistic works may be displayed or exhibited without permission because this does not infringe copyright.

Foreign material

All material from countries party to the Berne Convention should be given the same protection (national treatment) as UK material. Similarly, UK works are protected under the copyright laws of other Berne member states. However, the extension of the term of protection in EU member states for literary, dramatic, musical and artistic works for life plus 50 to 70 years has meant that most non EEA material will only be protected for the Berne minimum – 50 years. The US has now extended its term to 70 years. Some works in France have an extra nine years' protection to compensate authors for the period lost in the two World Wars. The UK does not recognize this extra term, so French works have the same protection as other EEA member states.

Free material

Material which is circulated free of charge – annual reports, brochures, press releases, leaflets etc. – is still protected by copyright although the copyright may be waived. Only copy in multiple with permission or obtain further copies. Permission would also be required for commercial exploitation.

Literacy hour

Many teachers are photocopying and enlarging complete texts for the whole class in the literacy hour. Many are also cutting up texts and making new or large editions with the children. It is advised that this practice may be infringing copyright, and should only be undertaken if permission has been given by publishers or it is covered by a licence. Packages from educational publishers which already contain big books and overhead transparencies should not be enlarged further unless permission had been obtained.

Microforms

Microforms which reproduce an original work without amendment (for example, a microfilmed report) should be treated in the same way as the original. The microform is a copyright photograph, but with only a facsimile copy of works on it, and copies have no copyright in themselves. A microform publisher might own additional rights as editor or compiler of an anthology, in which case permission to copy may be necessary. Otherwise only the rights of the authors and publishers of the original works apply to ordinary-sized copying.

Mixed media packages

Each component has its own copyright but the publisher may make a blanket claim on the format of the package. Copying is restricted to the terms of the package deal, but remember also that copying from anything other than printed material would be an infringement.

Obtaining material for stock

Under S.41 of the Library Regulations, librarians are allowed to request items from another library to add to their collection. Copies may not be made from the library's own collection under this exception (see page 17 for the library regulation governing copying for stock). Where the request is for only one copy of an article, and for less than the whole or (a substantial) part of a published work, there is no requirement to obtain written permission. Copies required for library stock may be obtained from the BLDSC or from any other library. **NB** Copies obtained under the library or interlibrary document supply service, or under fair dealing, may not be subsequently donated to the library collection, as they will have been obtained, and must be used, for the purposes of research or private study only. Copies obtained for stock, **even though they are photocopies**, are legitimate copies, and may be placed in the library collection and lent out or copied under fair dealing.

Photographs

There are different rules regarding photographs depending on the relevant Copyright Act at the time of taking. Establishing whether an old photograph is out of copyright can therefore be difficult, and the problem is exacerbated by some confusion over the length of the copyright term and whether it has been published or not. The copyright in all photographs taken prior to 1912 has now expired. For those taken between 1 July 1912 and 1 June 1957, copyright expires 50 years from the end of the calendar year in which the photograph was taken. As from January 1996 in the UK, photographs, whether published or unpublished, created between 1 June 1957 and 1 August 1989, are protected for 70 calendar years from when the negative was taken (but not those covered by the Crown or international organizations copyright).

It is no longer true to say that all photographs taken prior to 1934 are out of copyright, since many of them may be the subject of revived rights, although determining who, if anyone, now owns the rights, is a specialist problem. The original rights holder (not Crown) would be 'the person who owned the film when the photograph was taken'. This wording causes great difficulty for trying to determine the rights holder, because it implies that ownership is defined in terms of a *natural person*, not a legal one such as a company or other form of corporate body, who were and usually are the owners of this kind of intellectual property. Where copyright has clearly expired, access to use may still be difficult, as the reproduction rights in the original image may be controlled by a private organization or picture library.

Note that photographers have a legal right to have a reasonably prominent credit whenever a work is published, exhibited or shown in a film or on television. This right does not apply to employees who take photographs under contract of employment, unless the employer allows them to retain their rights.

Playing music in educational establishments

Playing music, other than to an audience of teachers and students, counts as a 'public performance' and will need to be licensed. For example, aerobics classes for people not registered as students or employees of an institution would almost certainly constitute a public performance. Phonographic Performance Ltd (PPL) controls the public performance and broadcasting of its members' sound recordings. Members of PPL consist of most of the well-known recording companies, multinationals and independents, as well as a number of specialized repertoire producers. The Performing Right Society (PRS) controls the licensing for use of the composers' and music publishers' rights. So any school considering playing a sound recording in public may need a licence from both PPL and the PRS. Any establishment considering giving a concert of live music only, i.e. not using sound recordings, may need to have a licence from the PRS only. The costs for a one-off event are likely to be very modest. The PPL and the PRS will be pleased to discuss individual needs. PPL provides a very useful information sheet.

Profit basis

The Act's phrase 'established or conducted for profit' applies to the parent organizations as well as to the services themselves, but the term is not defined. It seems reasonable to assume that it means that the organization or service concerned has the objective of attaining an excess of income over expenditure. The mere selling of services to recover a proportion of the expenditure, or even all the direct costs, without covering overheads and without making a true surplus, would not be construed as 'established or conducted for profit'. If a service were split off as an independent business without subsidy, it would then become 'established or conducted for profit'.

Prohibitive statements

Many publications contain statements which seem to forbid any copying or lending. By purchasing them for the library, it could be said that librarians had entered into an 'implied contract' with the publishers. Where copying is permitted by the Act (e.g. under fair dealing or the library regulations) or under a licence, it is most unlikely that a rights owner would bring a claim of infringement of 'implied contract' to court because of some phrase which had been put on an item. The law on unfair contract terms could be used in defence in any case, should a need arise. In general, therefore, it is advised that prohibitive or restrictive phrases, which seek to limit copying or use of an item to a greater extent than statute, may be ignored. Only if conditions of sale were agreed, or a full contract were entered into, could a rights owner have a sound case on contractual grounds. Contract law can override statute law in such circumstances.

Those worried about conditions of sale and wishing to be safe could put standard phrases of their own on order forms, indicating that the item is required for a library and will be treated like the rest of the stock in accordance with statute, thus generating their own contractual arrangements. This advice also applies to the purchase of videos, sound recordings and CD-ROMs for lending for educational purposes.

Under the new database regulations, lawful users of a database are authorized to do anything necessary to enable them to access and use the contents whether under licence to use or not, and any term or condition in any contract which accompanies the database which purports to prohibit or restrict this lawful use can be ignored. Similarly, a contract may not restrict lawful users from extracting or reutilizing *insubstantial* parts of a database which has been made available to the public in any manner (see page 27).

With regard to lending, educational establishments are exempt from lending right, so any statement which restricts lending may also be ignored. It is advised that the lending of such material should be for an educational purpose, i.e. to support the curriculum, and that it should not be run as a commercial enterprise. (See also **Videos** on page 64.)

Seeking copyright permission

If, when permission is sought to copy, it proves impossible to trace the rights owner but it is reasonable to assume the copyright has expired or that the author, or authors, died over 70 years ago, and there is evidence that reasonable enquiry has been made, copying could take place. What constitutes *reasonable enquiry* would have to be decided in a court of law if the rightful owner chose to prosecute. The standards of conduct expected by the law for information professionals is likely to be higher than those for the ordinary member of the public. Accordingly, in ascertaining whether or not a work is truly anonymous, that copyright has expired, or that the author of a work has died, information professionals would be expected to be aware of, and make full use of, all sources of information appropriate to the nature of the rights required. Enquiries should be tempered by economic realities, and should be measured against the expected or probable value of the use envisaged by the person or establishment wishing to make use of a work of undetermined copyright status. Prosecutions for infringement can take place up to six years after the year of an alleged offence, so records of steps taken should be kept for seven years. If it is not reasonable to assume that a work is out of copyright and the quest for the rights holder proves unsuccessful, there is a higher risk if the work is copied, as this could be seen as an infringement. On the other hand, provided all the steps are taken as above, if a rights holder makes him or herself known and can prove that the work is rightfully theirs, then this could just be a matter of a retrospective payment.

Self-service copying machines and liability

The responsibility for any photocopying or scanning machine within the library premises rests with the librarian. Any infringement which occurs on such machines could therefore involve the library staff and the school if a case were brought to court. It is important, therefore, that every effort is made to instil respect and compliance for copyright in staff and other users. It is the LA's view that self-operated copying machines may continue to be housed in libraries, provided that the following measures are taken:

1 Prominent notices should be displayed alongside in a position such that users will find them difficult to ignore. The notices should make it clear that copyright is protected by law, should indicate what limits may be applied, and should advise users to ask staff for guidance when in doubt. (Laminated posters can be obtained from LAHQ, see page 75 for details.)
2 Similar information should be incorporated in publicity material or library user guides, and in the library's regulations.
3 User education and induction programmes should also cover copyright.
4 Library staff training programmes should include copyright, so that appropriate advice can be given to users.
5 Line managers responsible for library resources should be included in such programmes.

Management should also consider cautionary statements in staff conditions of service and library conditions of access. It is a matter of internal policy whether library staff should intervene if they observe apparent infringements, but the view of the LA is that the appropriate member(s) of staff should be informed. The ultimate responsibility is likely to rest with the head teacher, who will be responsible for the actions of the staff. However, the CLA licence does provide indemnity for copying as part of compliance with its terms.

Topic files

School librarians may, when it is not reasonably practicable to purchase a copy of the item concerned, copy an original which is kept wholly or mainly for reference on the premises in order to preserve that original. Hence it is the LA's view that, when a periodical is for reference only, selected articles of importance may be copied without permission and placed in topic files, provided the issue is out of print or otherwise not 'reasonably practicable to purchase'. Copies may also be made under the library regulations provided all the conditions are complied with (see page 18). For newspaper clipping files, the LA also considers that it is a reasonable practice to copy reverse sides when needs conflict, unless this is a sufficiently frequent occurrence to suggest a second subscription. If the school is licensed by the Newspaper Licensing Agency, then this will be covered anyway.

Trade marks

A trade mark is any sign that can distinguish the goods and services of one trader from the goods or services of another, and can be represented graphically. Such signs may include words, including personal names, designs, letters, and the shape of goods or their packaging. A trade mark is used as a marketing tool so that customers can recognize the product of a particular trader. Generally the problem with trade marks is where one trader infringes their use by passing another's trade mark off as his/her own. Trade mark owners have the remedy of suing for infringement of registered marks, or if the trade mark is not registered, they may bring a common law action for passing off. Although the trade mark could have copyright as an artistic work, in the case of copying for research, private study or educational purposes, the Library Association believes that trade mark owners are not likely to bring an action of copyright infringement.

Translations

Before any copyright work is translated, the copyright owner should be consulted. This is not only because of the requirement for permission but also because of the author's moral rights, which imply that the author should be made aware of a risk of misinterpretation. Translating a whole work means making an adaptation, which is an infringement. If permission is granted, then the copyright in the new work belongs to the translator, although the original copyright stays with the author. Translating extracts of a work for a non-commercial educational purpose would not normally require permission.

Unpublished works

In the 1989 Act, unpublished manuscripts were given copyright only until 50 years from the death of the author [S.12], not in perpetuity (or until publication) as in previous legislation. However, that material already in copyright when the Act came into force (i.e. works by an author who died before August 1989) remained in copyright until the end of 2039 [Sch.1 S.12(4)]. When the new regulations on extending the term of copyright were introduced, the basic rule was that anyone who qualified had their work protected for life plus 70 years. Copyright should not last any longer than life plus 70 years, nor should copyright protection be reduced. Therefore those authors of unpublished works who died well before 1969 would still only be protected until the end of 2039. Thus those who died after 1969 will have their works protected for life plus 70 years. For example, a work of an unpublished author who died in 1920 will remain in copyright until the end of 2039, and so would the work of any author who died before 1969. However, an unpublished author who died after 1969 will have copyright for the full life plus 70 years. For example, an author who died in 1980 would now have his/her work protected until 2050 (please refer also to advice on **Photographs** on page 59).

Videos

Provided they are used for instructional purposes, the Act allows commercially produced videos to be shown in educational establishments. So phrases such as 'licensed for home use only' or 'may not be performed in clubs, prisons or schools' may be ignored as long as the audience consists of students and those giving instruction only. Educational establishments may also lend videos as part of the curriculum. (See also **Off-air recording licensing schemes** on page 40.)

Visually impaired persons

There is no exception, at present, to allow copying of whole works for the visually impaired. In order to reproduce a document in Braille, on tape, or in a large-print version, permission has to be obtained first. There is a movement to try to change this situation. The RNIB and the National Federation of the Blind are part of EFPICC (UK) (see page 52), the campaign which is supporting an exception for copying for visually impaired persons in the draft European Council Directive on Harmonization of Copyright (see page 29).

Without having to ask permission it should be acceptable for a reader to use a machine which simply reads out text and where no fixed copy is made, as this is unlikely to infringe copyright. It seems reasonable, also, to copy under fair dealing or the library regulations if only one article or a reasonable amount is copied onto tape for a user's research or private study. Those with normal sight are able to copy for this purpose, so it could be seen to be implicit that those who have vision impairment could use an intermediary process to treat them in the same way, i.e. non-discriminatory. This practice seems fair and unlikely to be an infringement, but, as with all fair dealing or library regulations copying, only a court of law could judge whether this is so. Permission would still have to be obtained for copying a substantial amount.

Permission is given in the CLA Schools licence for the making of enlarged reproductions from CLA-licensed material for the use by partially sighted pupils or staff. The conditions are that: such copies may only be used by partially sighted pupils or staff; at least one copy of the original publisher's edition of the work must have been purchased by the licensed institution and be available to other pupils of the school; the material must not already be available in large-print format; and copies must be logged as enlarged photocopies when required as part of a record-keeping scheme. Licensed institutions are not allowed to make any more copies than are required for the purposes of instruction for partially sighted pupils or for use by partially sighted staff. As with other copying, this non-exclusive right does not extend to electronic storage or transmission. Also, enlarged photocopies made may not be edited or bound up in any way, or sold or published (even for non-commercial purposes).

The Music Publishers Association has recognized the needs of the partially sighted by giving permission to make large-print versions of printed music subject to certain conditions. Before the copy is made, the publisher of the original text must be contacted first for approval. The conditions are: that the music was legitimately obtained; that multiple copies are not made; and that the enlarged copies are not resold. If all these conditions are met to the satisfaction of the publisher, applicants will be provided with a sticker to place on the large print version verifying its legitimacy (see *Music in large print*. RNIB/Music Publishers' Association, 1994).

Works created under the terms of an employment contract

This can cause confusion and difficulties if the position on who owns copyright in a work created, either at work or in the employee's own time, is not absolutely clear. The Act says that copyright is first owned by the employer when a literary, dramatic, musical or artistic work is created by an employee. Whether this is defined as during working hours only or it also covers leisure time is debatable. Therefore, if an employee wishes to retain the copyright for a work created outside work time, it is advisable to establish what the conditions of employment are and, if necessary, negotiate with the employer first.

13 Case law

A selection of some of the relevant copyright infringement cases has been included here to give a flavour as well as an idea of copyright risks. Interesting foreign cases have also been included.

Artistic works

The Design and Artists Copyright Society (DACS) sued art publishers Thames and Hudson for failing to pay royalties for the reproduction of paintings belonging to the estate of the German painter Max Beckmann. DACS said they were trying to bring royalties in line with those for authors, film-makers and musicians. As a defence, the publishers claimed fair dealing for criticism and review and argued that having to pay royalties would double the price of art books. The DACS case collapsed, however, when Christiane Beckmann, the artist's granddaughter, failed to testify.

- 'Copyright threat to modern art books: fears grow that royalty payments will raise prices', *Sunday Telegraph*, 26 February 1995.
- 'Royalties victory for art publisher', *Sunday Telegraph*, 19 March 1995.

In the case of BBC v. Pally Screen Printing, the BBC made a claim that the defendants had infringed copyright in a picture of the Teletubbies in the June 1997 issue of the magazine *BBC Toybox* and were guilty of passing off. The defendants denied any copying and based their defence on S.51 of the Act – the exception for making or copying a design. They argued that the original drawings for the Teletubbies were made in order to make the puppets, so the drawings were designs. The judge agreed with the defendants, albeit reluctantly. The plaintiff's claim for passing off was also dismissed. It was thought that the public was probably unaware that the puppets were made or approved by the BBC

- 'Eh-Oh! It's off to court the Teletubbies go', *Paisner & Co IP briefing*, 17, Autumn 1998.

Artistic works: maps

In March 1995, Ordnance Survey successfully prosecuted two publishing companies – Streetwise Map and Guide Ltd, Norfolk, and Color Maps International, Norwich – for copying OS maps and incorporating them in their publications without licence.

- **OS press release**, 5 June 1995.

The Department of the Environment for Northern Ireland ordered the Automobile Association to pay an undisclosed sum after the latter admitted infringing Crown copyright in maps and towns in the province. The Ordnance Survey has a long-running claim with the AA over the alleged use of unlicensed town maps in its publications.
- 'AA admits breach of copyright in Ulster', *Times*, 4 July 1998, 26.

Artistic works: photographs

A Belfast photographer sued the publisher Vermilion (part of Random House) for infringement of his copyright and moral right of integrity after his award-winning 'Time for Peace' photograph was manipulated and used on the cover of a recipe book, *Recipes for peace*, without permission.
- 'Look what they've done to my photo!', *Journalist weekly*, 16 October 1995.

An ex-mayor of Tower Hamlets was fined and ordered to pay compensation costs to the photographer for illegally using his photograph in a political leaflet. The photograph had been lifted deliberately from a copy of the London Daily News and used to smear an opponent.
- 'Former Mayor fined for copyright breach', *British journal of photography*, **138** (6843), 24 October 1991.
- 'Ex Mayor of Tower Hamlets convicted over " political smear" leaflet', press release from *Stephens Innocent*, 16 October 1991.

In a case in New York, the Bridgeman Art Library sued the Canadian company Corel for copying images which Bridgeman claimed belonged to them. These images were photographic transparencies of works of art in the public domain. The alleged infringements occurred in the US, Canada and Great Britain. Despite Bridgeman having registered these images in the US as derivative works, Corel contested that Bridgeman had no valid copyright and that there was no evidence of copying. Most of the original works of art are owned by museums in the UK and the photographs were first published in the UK, so the applicable law was decided to be that of the UK. The crucial question was whether there was enough skill, judgement and labour expended to qualify these images for protection. This principle is exemplified in the observation by the Privy Council which states:

> It takes great skill, judgement and labour to produce a good copy by painting or to produce an enlarged photograph from a positive print . . . no-one would reasonably contend that the copy painting or enlargement was an 'original' artistic work in which the copier is entitled to claim copyright. Skill, labour or judgement merely in the process of copying cannot confer original-

ity . . . There must in addition be some element of material alteration or embellishment which suffices to make the totality of the work an original work.

Based on this it was judged that the images did not qualify for copyright protection under the UK Act as there was no evidence of embellishment or alteration to the works. The judge could not be persuaded either that there was originality in the photographic works. In this case the works were akin to a scientific process. The case was dismissed.
• **1998 US Dist. LEXIS 17920**, *SDNY*, 13 November 1998.

An image of a Potawatamie Indian was scanned from a photograph and turned into a prize-winning drawing called 'The Real West'. The Ontario Court of Justice in Canada ruled that this was an infringement of the copyright in the original photograph.
• **'Whose line is it anyway?'**, *Guardian online*, 26 September 1998, 10.

The advertising agency Saatchi, when refused permission to use a photograph used in a Ministry of Defence army recruitment campaign, superimposed a model's face on the original.
• **'This means war'**, *Computing*, 5 June 1997, 140.

Books and periodicals

Publishers Schofield and Sims, the owners of copyright in certain mathematics text-books, claimed damages from the Forest of Dean Council for infringement of copyright by Royal Forest of Dean College. The college was alleged to have made multiple copies from these books at a time when Gloucestershire County Council did not have a licence from the publishers to do so.
• **'School book rumpus'**, *Gloucester citizen*, 10 September 1990.

Publishers in the US – American Geophysical Union, Elsevier Science, Pergamon, Springer, Wiley and Academic Press – successfully sued Texaco for photocopying from their books and journals for their staff without permission. In the decision ruled in July 1992, despite the claim by Texaco that they were copying under fair use, the judge ruled that companies cannot copy articles for internal use without first obtaining permission and compensating the rights holders. An appeal was lodged in September 1992 but the ruling was upheld.
• **'Appeals Court upholds Texaco copyright ruling'**, *Bookseller*, 11 November 1994.
  NB The US term *fair use* is not quite the same as the UK s fair dealing but, never-theless, this is an important precedent with implications for profit-based organiza-tions.

In the now deemed classic case of Magill v. BBC, Independent Television Publications

Ltd and RTE, the European Commission ruled that the refusal of the television companies to grant Magill licences to produce a guide to TV listings was an abuse of their dominant position under Article 86 of the Treaty of Rome. The Commission found in Magill's favour and made an order for licences to be granted. The TV companies went to the European Court to appeal but the judgement was upheld.

- 'Magill Case result', *News for EUSIDIC members*, special edition, April 1995.

In the case brought against Kinko's Graphic Corporation, a nationwide chain of photocopying stores in the US, it was ruled that Kinko's infringed the copyright of certain publishers (Basic Books, HarperCollins, John Wiley & Sons, McGraw-Hill, Penguin USA, Prentice-Hall, Richard D. Irwin and William Morrow) by reproducing excerpts from books and selling them in anthologies for college students. Kinko's claimed that the photocopying was necessary for educational purposes and used fair use as a defence. This was ruled out by the judge, who maintained that the real purpose for copying was for commercial reasons, as a large portion of their earnings came from photocopying substantial portions of copyrighted material.

- 'Photocopying chain found in violation of copyright law', *The chronicle of higher education*, 3 April 1991.

The Copyright Licensing Agency, acting on behalf of publishers the Open University and Centaur Press, obtained a considerable financial settlement for unauthorized photocopying from Essenheath Ltd – the commercial arm of Greenwich College, an independent business college in London. The CLA hired a private investigator to enrol as a student and found evidence that the college had reproduced copyright material without permission or licence for use in course work by students. The college was ordered to take out a CLA licence.

In 1984 Manchester City Council was ordered to pay £75,000 for copyright infringement. The case was triggered by a supply teacher, who was astonished to find quantities of his own book in photocopied form in a school stock room.

- 'Private investigator helps CLA win settlement', *Bookseller*, 5 March 1993.
- 'In the twilight world of the copyright busters: Jonathan Croall reports on moves to crack down on illegal photocopying', *Guardian education*, 16 March 1993.

In September 1994, The Copyright Agency Ltd (the Australian CLA), acting on behalf of 12 academic publishers in Australia, brought a case against Victoria University of Technology for the practice of compiling course anthologies for students. The court in Sydney dismissed the case but the decision has since been overturned on appeal.

- 'VUT in court to defend textbook photocopying', *Australian*, 7 September 1994.
- 'Ruling will prove a death sentence to our wordsmiths', *Australian*, 9 November 1994.

The CLA and four publishers were successful in taking Dar Al Handasah, a firm of engineering consultants, plus two other named defendants to the High Court for infringing copyright in their publications. The case was initiated as part of the Copywatch campaign whereby a former employee 'blew the whistle' on them to the CLA.

- **CLA news release**, December 1996.

In South Africa's first major copyright infringement case to reach court, a branch of the copy shop Prontaprint was found guilty and fined for unauthorized multiple copying of 54 book titles. The case was brought by the CLA-equivalent company DALRO (Dramatic, Artistic and Literary Rights Organization).

- **'SA court imposes heavy fine in copyright infringement case'**, *The Bookseller*, 12 April 1996, 11.

A copy shop in Store Street, London, was found to be copying large excerpts of works for course packs used by students at SOAS. The shop had to pay substantial costs and agreed to take out a CLA licence.

- **'Copyright course packs exposed'**, *The Bookseller*, 15 November 1996, 8.
- **'Authors lose £££s in copy scam'**, *Times higher*, 8 November 1996, 3.

In a case sponsored by the Association of American Publishers, a US court judge ruled that a US copy-shop chain, Michigan Document Services, must obtain permission from rights holders and pay fees when using substantial extracts of copyright material in their course packs.

- **'US publishers in landmark copyshop victory'**, *The Bookseller*, 29 November 1996, 11.
- **'Publishers win important fair use victory'**, *AAP news release*, 11 November 1996.

The author, Janet Dailey, admitted plagiarizing plots and copying passages from a rival romantic fiction author, Nora Roberts. Discussions took place out of court.

- **'Romantic friction as author admits copying her rival'**, *Daily Telegraph*, 1 August 1997, 17.

An unnamed firm of chartered accountants was issued with a writ and successfully sued for heavy damages by Fenman, the publisher of a loose-leaf training manual, when a member of staff made an illegal photocopy of the manual and left incriminating evidence to the effect.

- **Training Media Copyright Association website: http://www.tcma.org/** (accessed December 1998).

Newspapers

NLA successfully sued Marks and Spencer for making, and distributing internally, unlicensed copies from newspapers. M&S used the defence of fair dealing for news reporting, which of course does not cover the typographical arrangement.

- 'Newspapers defeat M&S on copyright', *Daily Telegraph*, 20 January 1999.
- 'Circulating press cuttings went beyond fair dealing', *Times*, 26 January 1999, 4.

The NLA also sued Islington Borough Council for copyright infringement because the Council refused to pay licence invoices.

- 'Council sued for copyright infringement', *Press gazette*, 4 September 1998, 2.

The Copyright Tribunal were invoked to give a decision on a dispute between Romeike and Curtice, a press cuttings agency, and the Newspaper Licensing Agency regarding a clause in the NLA licence which obliged licensees to disclose client names to the NLA, or stop supplying cuttings to clients if they do not acknowledge in writing within a specified period that they will not make further copies of licensed items. R&C claimed administrative burden and said that the clause was unreasonable and would seriously offend clients. The Tribunal, in its interim decision, ruled that as a term of the licence there should be an endorsement on each cutting to the effect that no further copying should take place unless authorized by statute. Also, the licensee should write to each client drawing attention to copyright compliance and the necessity of having an NLA licence. If the licensee became aware of an client infringing newspaper then they would have to disclose the client corporate name to the NLA.

- Romeike and Curtice Ltd -v- Newspaper Licensing Agency Ltd, interim decision 3 August 1998 (copies of decisions available from Patent Office; see also www.patent.gov.uk/dpolicy/recent.html).

Computer software

Following proceedings against the London Borough of Greenwich by the Federation Against Software Theft and the Business Software Alliance on behalf of Lotus and Xtree, an out-of-court settlement was agreed. Illegal software was found in the Housing Directorate.

- 'Greenwich faces FAST software theft charge', *Computer weekly*, 12 December 1991.
- 'London Borough of Greenwich and software publishers agree out of court settlement in software copying case', Greenwich Council press release, 10 January 1992.

Music and sound recordings

The Royal Ulster Constabulary Male Voice Choir had to pay £2,000 damages and costs

to the Music Publishers Association for photocopying scores.
- 'Not so happy', *Independent*, 13 June 1992.

A religious publisher, OCP of Portland Oregon, sued the producers of the Princess Diana memorial CD for including a track of a hymn without permission.
- 'Court battle on Diana CD', *The Mail on Sunday*, 2 November 1997.

Videos

An English language school in York illicitly copied 300 videos. The school paid £71,000 in an out-of-court settlement.
- 'In the twilight world of the copyright busters: Jonathan Croall reports on moves to crack down on illegal photocopying', *Guardian education*, 16 March 1993.

In June 1994 Bayer plc was successfully sued by Video Arts for pirating one of its sales training programmes. Bayer had to pay £20,000 fine and was ordered not to infringe in future.
- Training Media Copyright Association website: http://www.tcma.org/ (accessed December 1998).

Performance right

A cinema manageress was convicted of copyright infringement for screening Stanley Kubrick's film *A clockwork orange* in Britain. The film had been banned by Kubrick himself, who was exercising his moral right of disclosure. The case was brought by the Federation Against Copyright Theft (FACT). The film used was a pirated video.
- 'Cinema boss accused over Clockwork Orange showing', *Daily Telegraph*, 5 February 1993.
- 'Clockwork Orange woman pays £1000: Kubrick s banned film depicting teenage violence returns after 20 years to spark fresh controversy', *Daily Telegraph*, 24 March 1993.
- 'Kubrick screening breached copyright', *Guardian*, 24 March 1993.

Rental right

The British Phonographic Industry was granted an injunction to prevent an Eastbourne store, Satin Sounds, from renting out CDs and music videos.
- 'Trade faces the music', *Video business*, 9 February, 1991.

Digital works

Jonathan Tasini, President of the New York-based National Writers Union, and nine other writers sued database operators Mead Data Central (owned by Reed Elsevier) and three major publishers, the New York Times Corporation, the Times–Mirror Corporation and the Time Warner Corporation, for using their articles in an online database without permission or payment. The National Union of Journalists was also concerned about a number of UK publishers who put their work online without permission or payment. The case was settled in 1997. The judge threw out the writers' case on the grounds that the US Copyright Act allows the publisher of a collective work (such as a magazine or newspaper) to reuse contributions 'in any revision of that collective work'. However, both sides agree that such sub-licensing must be made more clear-cut.

- 'Copyright reservations', *Guardian*, 8 June 1995.
- 'First U.S. Court decisions on electronic rights: what next?', *ASJA contracts watch* 49, 4 (10), 15 August 1997.

Over 20 MIDI sound files containing copies of songs from film soundtracks and recording artists were found on an area for personal web pages on a university web server. The rights holders objected and the material was removed.

- 'E-mail from UKERNA', cert@cert.ja.net, February 1996.

The launch of a German-produced CD-ROM containing a 'reverse search' version of the entire BT telephone directory was blocked in the High Court because BT claimed that the German company, Top Ware, was breaching copyright. The disc, called 'UK-Info', was planned to be sold in the UK at £19.95 against the price charged for the BT version of £199. The BT version does not allow 'reverse searching' because of data protection considerations.

- 'BT in a spin over CD-Rom directory', *Independent*, 10 September 1996, 6.
- 'Court blocks phone directory on disc', *Independent*, 21 September 1996, 4.

The *Shetland Times* brought a case against a fellow online newspaper, *Shetland News*, for providing direct hypertext links to news items on its site and so bypassing its homepage. Readers of *Shetland News* were unaware that they were reading items from *Shetland Times*. The *Shetland Times* based its case on hypertext links being a breach of copyright. The case was settled out of court in November 1997, so not proven, although *Shetland News* was ordered to acknowledge all links.

- http://www.shetland-news.co.uk/headline/97nov/settled.html
- www.shetland-times.co.uk/st/daily/dispute.html (accessed 14 November 1997).
- 'Shetland settlement fails to defuse row', *Press gazette*, 21 November 1997, 10.
- 'Shetland Times Ltd. v. Dr Jonathan Wills and Another', SCLR **160**, 1996.
- Connolly J. P. et al, 'Fair Dealing in Webbed Links of Shetland Yarns', *Journal of*

Information law and technology (JILT), 1998 (2) (**http://elj.warwick.ac.uk/jilt/copyright/98 _2conn/**).

Dutch public libraries were prevented from producing a CD-ROM containing clippings of literary reviews, many of which were by freelance contributors, without permission. The libraries claimed that their right to disseminate information freely was impeded.

- **'Freelancers assert their rights: Newspaper Web sites and copyrights: cases pending'**, *Information world review*, May 1998, 20.

14 Other LA Copyright Guides and posters

The Library Association Copyright Guides

The following similar guides are published by Library Association Publishing at £9.95 each:

Copyright in further and higher education libraries (ISBN 1-85604-322-3)
Copyright in health libraries (ISBN 1-85604-323-1)
Copyright in industrial and commercial libraries (ISBN 1-85604-324-X)
Copyright in public libraries (ISBN 1-85604-325-8)
Copyright in voluntary sector libraries (ISBN 1-85604-327-4)

They are available from: Bookpoint Ltd, Mail Order Department, 39 Milton Park, Abingdon, Oxon OX14 4TD. Tel: (01235) 827794; Fax: (01235) 400454; e-mail: orders@bookpoint.co.uk.

Posters

The Library Association has produced two attractive A3-size laminated posters: a warning poster advising on what may be copied safely, intended for display beside photocopying and optical scanning machines; and another on downloading from portable databases and copying from the Internet for displaying next to computer terminals. Each poster costs: £4.00 (non-members £5.00) for up to nine copies; £3.50 (£4.50 non-members) for 10 or more. Payment may be made by sending a cheque with order, or if that is not convenient, a pro-forma invoice may be sent on receipt of an order. Cheques should be made payable to The Library Association. Orders should be sent to: COPYRIGHT POSTERS, Information Services, The Library Association, 7 Ridgmount Street, London WC1E 7AE. It would also be helpful if an adhesive self-addressed label could be sent with orders.

Appendix A Prescribed libraries and archives

1 **Public libraries:**
Any library administered by
* a public library authority in England and Wales
* a statutory library authority in Scotland
* an Education and Library Board in Northern Ireland.

2 **National libraries:**
* British Library
* National Library of Wales
* National Library of Scotland
* Bodleian Library, Oxford
* University Library, Cambridge.

3 **Libraries in educational establishments:**
* a library of a school
* libraries of universities which are empowered to award degrees
* libraries of institutions providing further or higher education.

4 **Parliamentary and government libraries**

5 **Local government libraries:**
Any library administered by
* a local authority in England and Wales
* a local authority in Scotland
* a district council in Northern Ireland.

6 **Other libraries:**
* Any library which encourages the study of bibliography, education, fine arts, history, languages, law, literature, medicine, music, philosophy, religion, science (including natural and social science) or technology
* Any library outside the UK which encourages the study of the above subjects.

Source: **SI 1989:1068** and **SI 1989:1212**

Appendix B   Prescribed copyright declaration form

DECLARATION: COPY OF ARTICLE OR PART OF PUBLISHED WORK [1]

To: The Librarian of [...] Library [Address of Library]

Please supply me with a copy of [2]
the article in the periodical, the particulars of which are [   ]
the part of the published work, the particulars of which are [   ]
required by me for the purposes of research or private study.

I declare that

(a) I have not previously been supplied with a copy of the same material by you or any other librarian;
(b) I will not use the copy except for research or private study and will not supply a copy of it to any other person; and
(c) to the best of my knowledge no other person with whom I work or study has made or intends to make, at or about the same time as this request, a request for substantially the same material for substantially the same purpose.

I understand that if the declaration is false in a material particular the copy supplied to me by you will be an infringing copy and that I shall be liable for infringement of copyright as if I had made the copy myself.

Signature [3] ....
Date ....
Name ....
Address ....
....
....

---

1 A similar declaration form for unpublished works is also to be found in SI 1989:1212.
2 Delete whichever is inappropriate.
3 This must be the personal signature of the person making the request. A stamped or typewritten signature, or the signature of an agent, is *not* acceptable.

Appendix C   Some useful addresses

British Copyright Council, Copyright House, 29–33 Berners Street, London W1P 4AA. [mailing address]
Tel: (01986) 788122; fax: (01986) 788847; e-mail: copyright@bcc2.demon.co.uk

British Music Rights, British Music House, 26 Berners Street, London W1P 3DB.
Tel: 020 7306 4446; fax: 020 7306 4449; e-mail: britishmusic@bmr.org;
http://www.bmr.org.

British Photographers' Liaison Committee (incorporating The Committee on Photographic Copyright), 81 Leonard Street, London EC2A 4QS.
Tel: 020 7739 6669; fax: 020 7739 8707.

The British Phonographic Industry, 25 Savile Row, London W1X 1AA.
Tel: 020 7287 4422; fax: 020 7734 2015; http://www.bpi.co.uk

British Standards Institution, 389 Chiswick High Road, London W4 4AL.
Tel: 020 8996 9000; fax: 020 8996 7400; e-mail: info@bsi.org.uk;
http://www.bsi.org.uk/.

Christian Copyright Licensing International (CCLI), PO Box 1339, Eastbourne, East Sussex BN21 4SA.
Tel: 01323 417711; fax: 01323 417722; e-mail: info@ccli.co.ul.

Copyright Licensing Agency, 90 Tottenham Court Road, London W1P 9HE.
Tel: 020 7631 5555; fax: 020 7631 5500; e-mail: cla@cla.co.uk; http://www.cla.co.uk.

Design and Artists Copyright Society, Parchment House, 13 Northburgh Street, London EC1V 0AH.
Tel: 020 7336 8811; fax: 020 7336 8822; e-mail:info@dacs.co.uk.

Educational Recording Agency, New Premier House, 150 Southampton Row, London WC1B 5AL.
Tel: 020 7837 3222; fax: 020 7837 3750; e-mail: era@era.org.uk;
http://www.era.org.uk.

European Bureau of Library and Information Documentation Associations (EBLIDA), PO Box 43300, NL-2504 AH The Hague, The Netherlands.
Tel: (+31) 70-309 06 08; fax: (+31)70-309 07 08; e-mail: eblida@nblc.nl;
http://www.eblida.org/.

HMSO Copyright Unit, St Clements House, 2–16 Colegate, Norwich NR3 1BQ.
Tel: (01603) 723001; fax: (01603) 723000; http://www.hmso.gov.uk/copy.htm.

The Library Association, 7 Ridgmount Street, London WC1E 7AE.
Tel: 020 7636 7543; fax: 020 7436 7218; e-mail: info@la-hq.org.uk; http://www.la-hq.org.uk.

The LA/JCC Working Party on Copyright, c/o The Library Association (as above).

The LA/JCC Working Party on Copyright, c/o The Library Association (as above).

Mechanical Copyright Protection Society, Copyright House, 29–33 Berners Street, London W1P 4AA.
  Tel: 020 7580 5544; fax: 020 7306 4455; e-mail: info@mcps.co.uk; http://www.mcps.co.uk.

Music Publishers' Association Ltd, 3rd Floor, Strand Gate, 18–20 York Buildings, London WC2N 6JU.
  Tel: 020 7839 7779; fax: 020 7839 7776; e-mail: mpa@musicpublishers.co.uk.

Newspaper Licensing Agency Ltd, Lonsdale Gate, Lonsdale Gardens, Tunbridge Wells, Kent TN1 1NL.
  Tel: (01892) 525273; fax: (01892) 525275; e-mail: copy@nla.co.uk; http://www.nla.org.uk.

Office for Official Publications of the European Communities, 2 rue de Mercier, L2985 Luxembourg.
  Tel: (+352) 499 28 2565; fax: (+352) 499 10 62 16.

Open University Educational Enterprises Ltd, 12 Cofferidge Close, Stony Stratford, Milton Keynes MK11 1BY.
  Tel: (01908) 261662; e-mail: OUEEEnq@open.ac.uk.

Ordnance Survey, Copyright Branch, Romsey Road, Maybush, Southampton SO9 4DH.
  Tel: (01703) 792706; fax: (01703) 792535.

The Patent Office, Copyright Directorate, 25 Southampton Buildings, London WC2A 1AY. From 14 June 1999 the address will be: Harmsworth House, 13-15 Bouverie Street, London EC4Y 8DP.
  Tel: 020 7438 4777; fax: 020 7448 4780/4713; e-mail: copyright@patent.gov.uk.

Performing Right Society, Copyright House, 29–33 Berners Street, London W1P 4AA.
  Tel: 020 7580 5544; fax: 020 7306 4455; e-mail: info@prs.co.uk; http://www.prs.co.uk.

Phonographic Performance Ltd, Ganton House, 14–22 Ganton Street, London W1V 1LB.
  Tel: 020 7437 0311; fax: 020 7534 1111; e-mail: postmaster@ppluk.demon.co.uk.

Video Performance Ltd, same address and telephone as Phonographic Performance Ltd (see above).

World Intellectual Property Organization, 34 Chemin des Columbettes, 1211 Geneva 20, Switzerland.
  Tel: (+41) 22 338 9111; fax: (+41) 22 733 5428; e-mail: COPYRIGHT.mail@wipo.int http://www.wipo.int

Statutory material and further reading

Please note that since 1997 all new Statutory Instruments are published in full-text form on the HMSO web pages.

Berne Convention for the Protection of Literary and Artistic Works, Paris Act 1971. WIPO, Geneva, 1989.

Copyright, Designs and Patents Act 1988. HMSO. ISBN 0 10 544888 5. Price: £12.50.

The Copyright (Educational Establishments) (No 2) Order 1989. SI 1990:1068. HMSO. ISBN 0 11 097068 3. Price: £0.50.

The Copyright (Librarians and Archivists) (Copying of Copyright Material) Regulations 1989. SI 1989:1212. HMSO. ISBN 0 11 097212 0. Price: £1.65.

The Copyright (Computer Programs) Regulations 1992. SI 1992:3233. HMSO. ISBN 0 11 025116 4. Price: £1.50.

The Duration of Copyright and Rights in Performances Regulations 1995. SI 1995:3297. HMSO. ISBN 0 11 053833 1. Price: £3.70.

The Copyright and Related Rights Regulations 1996. SI 1996:2967. The Stationery Office Ltd. ISBN 0 11 063334 2. Price £4.70.

The Copyright and Rights in Databases Regulations 1997. SI 1997:3032. The Stationery Office Ltd. ISBN 0 11 065325 4. Price £3.20.

The Future Management of Crown Copyright. Cm 4300. The Stationery Office Ltd. ISBN 0 10 143002 7. Price: £9.50. (Also available at **http://www.hmso.gov.uk/document/copywp.htm**).

Proposal for a European Parliament and Council Directive on the harmonization of certain aspects of copyright and related rights in the Information Society (COM (97) 628 final) 10 December 1997. **http://europa.eu.int/comm/dg15/en/index.htm**.

WIPO Copyright Treaty, Geneva 1996. **www.wipo.int**.

The ABC of UK photographic copyright, British Photographers Liaison Committee, 1994. ISBN 0 9514671 1 5 (presently being revised).

Copyright guidelines for JISC and TLTP projects (Joint Information Systems Committee and Teaching and Learning Technology Programme) Electronic Libraries Programme Studies, 1998. ISBN 1 9500508 41 9

Cornish, G. P., *Copyright: interpreting the law for libraries, archives and information services*, 3rd edn, Library Association Publishing, 1999. ISBN 1 85604 344 4.

Licensing digital resources: how to avoid the legal pitfalls?, ECUP/EBLIDA, 1998. **www.eblida/ecup/docs/warning.html**.

Music in large print, RNIB/Music Publishers' Association, 1994. ISBN 185878 026 8.

Norman, S., '*Report of the WIPO Diplomatic Conference, 2–20 December 1996*', *IFLA journal*, **23** (2), 1997, 136–9.

Pedley, P., *Copyright for library and information services professionals*, Aslib, 1998. ISBN 0 85142 412 0.

Phillips, J. (managing editor), Wall, R. and Oppenheim, C. (eds.), *Aslib guide to copyright*, Aslib, 1994. ISBN 0 851 42 311 6 (loose-leaf, available on subscription).

Post, J. B. and Foster, M. R., *Copyright: a handbook for archivists*, Society of Archivists, 1992. ISBN 0 902 886 43 6 (needs to be revised, but still useful).

Report of the Joint Information Systems Committee & Publishers Association Working Party on fair dealing in an electronic environment (JISC/PA), 1997. **www.ukoln.ac.uk/services/elib/papers/pa/**.

Wall, R. A., *Copyright made easier*, Aslib, 1998. ISBN 0 85142 393 0.

Index